Schöningh

EinFach Englisch

Tennessee Williams

A Streetcar Named Desire

Edited by
Peter Noçon

Series Editor:
Hans Kröger

Sprachliche Betreuung: Alexandra Rieb/www.arlanguages.com

www.schoeningh-schulbuch.de
Schöningh Verlag, Jühenplatz 1–3, 33098 Paderborn

Druck A 7 6 5 / Jahr 2018 17 16
Alle Drucke der Serie A sind im Unterricht parallel verwendbar.
Die letzte Zahl bezeichnet das Jahr dieses Druckes.

Umschlaggestaltung: Jennifer Kirchhof
Umschlagabbildung: © action press/EVERETT COLLECTION, INC
Druck und Bindung: westermann druck GmbH, Braunschweig

ISBN 978-3-14-041192-9

Contents

Getting started

Compare the two stills from Elia Kazan's film version (l.) and John Erman's TV version (r.) of *A Streetcar Named Desire* and describe the atmosphere evoked by them.

A Note on the Text

The text of the play is that of the first American edition (1947), reissued by New Directions in 2004. The standard British edition was published by Secker & Warburg in 1957 as *Four Plays by Tennessee Williams.* The English edition varies from the original edition in several instances and, generally, conforms to British spelling and usage, which, on occasion, seems to alter the Southern background and the atmosphere Tennessee Williams clearly wants to evoke. To keep as close as possible to the author's intention, then, the play ought to be spoken with an American accent, or, more precisely, the various dialects and sociolects of American English (General American, Southern speech, Mexican American, Black English) should be used when staging the play. In keeping with the practice of most school editions, the annotations here follow British standards. The pronunciation aids provided for difficult words conform to British English usage, but note is taken of widely differing American pronunciations.

How to Read a Play

The text of a play lives a double life – in the playhouse and on paper.
In a performance-oriented approach to play-reading, the following aspects should be considered:

- The text is a script that comes alive only in performance (like a musical score).
- Hence, a play is designed for the stage, and a performance is a coproduction of writer, director, actors, electricians, stage designers, costume designers etc.
- The text of a play consists of dialogue (text) and stage directions (subtext). Being a script, it calls for the director to interpret it and, possibly, alter it in moderation (e.g. adapt it to modern circumstances).
- The director is restricted by the physical conditions of the stage available (e.g. a performance on a picture-frame stage is bound to be a different experience from one in a theatre-in-the-round).
- Decisions have to be taken about décor, lighting (e.g. spotlighting), sound effects and costume (e.g. do the actors wear historical or modern dress?).
- Actors have to be chosen and assigned their roles (in most cases, the director has a group of actors who are closely associated with a theatre or employed by a company; occasionally, though, there is auditioning for a certain play and the director has a choice).
- Actors have to play their roles with close attention to enunciation and voice (e.g. pitch, tempo, modulation)
  posture
  facial expression
  gesture
  movement

In brief, speech and body language are equally important.

When reading a play, readers have to cast themselves as directors who want to make the words happen on stage. Unlike the audience in a theatre, they can stop at certain places in the text and check on what they have read or reflect on it and, clearly, a play needn't be read in one sitting. But readers have to visualize what is going on in a play on much flimsier evidence than they have when reading a novel. The text of a play has many gaps for the reader to fill. Thus, the reading of a play not only requires close attention but also the exercise of the reader's imagination. Even if you read a play as a literary text, you are obliged to bear in mind the play's theatrical dimension:

- Readers should read up on the historical, political, social and cultural background which informs the play.
- They have to consider both dialogue or monologue and the author's stage directions. Over and above the express information given, the dialogue may contain a certain undertone (e.g. of irony or menace) while the stage directions may include an author's interpretative comments which may very well go far beyond mere directions to actors.
- Readers have to picture a setting for the evolving action. Usually, the stage directions give adequate hints in this respect; furthermore, the dialogue itself may include indications as to place and time.
- Plays generally follow a traditional model of act and scene division. Readers have to look out for a pattern. They will have to note exits and entrances and remember that the absence of a character in a scene may be as important as their presence.
- Readers have to form for themselves a picture of the characters interacting in the play. How do they relate to other characters? How stable is that relationship? Are there clearcut protagonists and antagonists? Are the characters lifelike or stock characters, mere cardboard figures? Do they develop in the course of the action? How do they speak? What kind of language do they use in a given situation? For instance, do they speak differently to different characters or in different situations? Do they use marked language such as slang on the one hand, or formal language on the other? Do the characters belong to different layers of society? What is made of gender in the play? Does the author want you to identify with one of the characters (which you, of course, may refuse to do) or does he/she have the same extent of sympathy for all the characters?
- The backbone of a play is its action, which is shaped into a plot with a beginning, middle and end in the Aristotelian sense. (This does not mean that the play's action has to follow a chronological order; it may work back from the ending, as in analytical plays; it may freely switch to and fro from one time level to another; it may have flashforwards and flashbacks, called prolepsis and analepsis in technical language.) However, the action is always predicated on conflict which, in drama, is generally between two sets of people. The action may arrive at a satisfactory conclusion (closure), or it may be open-ended; it may be linear (teleological, that is, inexorably

directed towards an end) or circular (cyclical, that is, turning upon itself and returning to the beginning with no progress at all). Note that, in the linear plot, we usually have an exposition, developing action, climax or turning-point/peripeteia and resolution/denouement. Obviously, in a circular or static plot the above-mentioned phases in the construction of a plot do not occur, so that, strictly speaking, plot is a misnomer here, for nothing seems to happen.
- Finally, readers will have to come to a decision about the overall meaning of a play. Does it make a statement about life/ about society etc.? Is it tragic, tragicomic or absurd? Does the play meet your expectations? Does it affect you in any way and does it make you think about the problems posed by the play? Is it entertaining, and possibly only intended as entertainment, or does it have an overt message?

Like a theatre audience, readers are expected to engage with a play. Of course, your response should be personal, and you may very well voice your own opinion of it as long as you are willing to check your ideas against what happens in the text or on the stage.

List of Characters

Blanche Dubois [blæntʃ du'bɔɪs] in Elia Kazan's film it is [du'bwɑ:]

Eunice ['ju:nɪs]

BLANCHE DUBOIS
STELLA KOWALSKI
STANLEY KOWALSKI
HAROLD MITCHELL (MITCH)
EUNICE HUBBELL
STEVE HUBBELL
PABLO GONZALES
A NEGRO WOMAN
A DOCTOR
A NURSE
A YOUNG COLLECTOR
A MEXICAN WOMAN
A TAMALE VENDOR

A Streetcar Named Desire

And so it was I entered the broken world
To trace the visionary company of love, its voice
An instant in the wind (I know not whither hurled)
But not for long to hold each desperate choice.

"The Broken Tower" by Hart Crane

➊ What does the epigraph say? Bear it in mind while you read the play.

whither (old-fashioned) where to

"The Broken Tower" The epigraph is the fifth stanza (out of ten) of Hart Crane's last poem, written in Mexico in the spring of 1932, shortly before he committed suicide. Hart Crane was an important American poet (1899–1932) whose poetry often defied easy interpretation.

Scene One

Separate those elements from the stage directions that can easily be put on stage from those that suggest mood and atmosphere. What can the director of a play do in such a case? To what extent does he depend on stage designers, electricians etc.?

The exterior of a two-story corner building on a street in New Orleans which is named Elysian Fields and runs between the L & N tracks and the river. The section is poor but, unlike corresponding sections in other American cities, it has a raffish charm. The houses are mostly white frame, weathered gray, with rickety outside stairs and galleries and quaintly ornamented gables. This building contains two flats, upstairs and down. Faded white stairs ascend to the entrances of both.

It is first dark of an evening early in May. The sky that shows around the dim white building is a peculiarly tender blue, almost a turquoise, which invests the scene with a kind of lyricism and gracefully attenuates the atmosphere of decay. You can almost feel the warm breath of the brown river beyond the river warehouses with their faint redolences of bananas and coffee. A corresponding air is evoked by the music of Negro entertainers at a barroom around the corner. In this part of New Orleans you are practically always just around the corner, or a few doors down the street, from a tinny piano being played with the infatuated fluency of brown fingers. This "blue piano" expresses the spirit of the life which goes on here.

Two women, one white and one colored, are taking the air on the steps of the building. The white woman is Eunice, who occupies the upstairs flat; the colored woman a neighbor, for New Orleans is a cosmopolitan city where there is a relatively warm and easy intermingling of races in the old part of town.

Above the music of the "blue piano" the voices of people on the street can be heard overlapping.

[*Two men come around the corner, Stanley Kowalski and Mitch. They are about twenty-eight or thirty years old, roughly dressed in blue denim work clothes. Stanley carries his bowling jacket and a red-stained package from a butcher's. They stop at the foot of the steps.*]

STANLEY [*bellowing*] Hey, there! Stella, Baby!

[*Stella comes out on the first floor landing, a gentle young woman, about twenty-five, and of a background obviously quite different from her husband's.*]

STELLA [*mildly*] Don't holler at me like that. Hi, Mitch.

STANLEY Catch!

STELLA What?

STANLEY Meat!

[*He heaves the package at her. She cries out in protest but manages to catch it: then she laughs breathlessly. Her husband and his companion have already started back around the corner.*]

Elysian Fields [ɪ'lɪziən] a street in New Orleans; in Greek mythology, Elysium is the place of perfect happiness
L&N the Louisville and Nashville Line (railroad)
raffish having a carelessly unconventional style; rakish
white frame a house made of wooden planks and painted white
rickety shaky
quaint old-fashioned in a charming and endearing way
gable *Giebel*
peculiar odd, strange
turquoise ['tɜːkwɔɪz] greenish blue
attenuate to lessen in severity or intensity; to weaken
warehouse a building where goods are stored before distribution or are kept in reserve (Careful! The German word "*Warenhaus*" is a false friend: "department store").
redolence ['redələns] sweet-smelling fragrance
tinny *blechern*
infatuated [in'fætʃueɪtɪd] completely carried away by love (here: love in one's own skill)
"Blue" Piano blues (slow and melancholy jazz music) played on a piano
intermingling mixing together easily
overlapping *überlappend*
denim [denɪm] coarse, sturdy cotton cloth used for jeans
bellow to shout, to roar
landing a platform at the end of a flight of stairs
holler to shout, to yell
heave (here) to throw sth heavy (informal use)

STELLA [*calling after him*] Stanley! Where are you going?

STANLEY Bowling!

STELLA Can I come watch?

STANLEY Come on. [*He goes out.*]

STELLA Be over soon. [*To the white woman*] Hello, Eunice. How are you?

EUNICE I'm all right. Tell Steve to get him a poor boy's sandwich 'cause nothing's left here.

[*They all laugh; the colored woman does not stop. Stella goes out.*]

COLORED WOMAN What was that package he th'ew at 'er?

[*She rises from steps, laughing louder.*]

EUNICE You hush, now!

NEGRO WOMAN Catch *what*!

[*She continues to laugh. Blanche comes around the corner, carrying a valise. She looks at a slip of paper, then at the building, then again at the slip and again at the building. Her expression is one of shocked disbelief. Her appearance is incongruous to this setting. She is daintily dressed in a white suit with a fluffy bodice, necklace and earrings of pearl, white gloves and hat, looking as if she were arriving at a summer tea or cocktail party in the garden district. She is about five years older than Stella. Her delicate beauty must avoid a strong light. There is something about her uncertain manner, as well as her white clothes, that suggests a moth.*]

EUNICE [*finally*] What's the matter, honey? Are you lost?

BLANCHE [*with faintly hysterical humor*] They told me to take a street-car named Desire, and then transfer to one called Cemeteries and ride six blocks and get off at – Elysian Fields!

From Elia Kazan's film (1951)

poor boy's sandwich (also, poor boy sandwich, hero sandwich) a sandwich made of a large roll sliced lengthwise and filled with cold meats, cheeses and vegetables

valise [və'li:z] (old-fashioned) a piece of hand luggage

incongruous [ɪn'kɒŋgruəs] unsuitable, not corresponding to what is right or customary

dainty showing refined taste, almost excessively so

fluffy very soft, feathery

bodice the upper part of a woman's dress

garden district a residential area for rich people in New Orleans, southwest of the old city (Vieux Carré)

In what way does Blanche seem to be different from the characters surrounding her?

street-car (also, streetcar) a car on rails for public transport (the British equivalent is "tram"; in New Orleans, streetcars began running in the 1920s; the "streetcar named Desire" stopped operating in 1948)

Desire the terminal stop is in a quarter called "Desire" (a desire is a strong wish or craving)

Cemeteries ['semətriz] another streetcar line having "Cemeteries" as its terminal stop (a cemetery is a graveyard)

EUNICE That's where you are now.

BLANCHE At Elysian Fields?

EUNICE This here is Elysian Fields.

BLANCHE They mustn't have – understood – what number I wanted …

EUNICE What number you lookin' for?

[*Blanche wearily refers to the slip of paper.*]

BLANCHE Six thirty-two.

EUNICE You don't have to look no further.

uncomprehending not understanding what is going on

BLANCHE [*uncomprehendingly*] I'm looking for my sister, Stella DuBois. I mean – Mrs. Stanley Kowalski.

EUNICE That's the party. – You just did miss her, though.

BLANCHE This – can this be – her home?

EUNICE She's got the downstairs here and I got the up.

BLANCHE Oh. She's – out?

bowling alley a building with a number of lanes used for bowling (game in which a heavy ball is bowled along a lane in order to knock over ten wooden pins that are set upright at the far end of the lane)

EUNICE You noticed that bowling alley around the corner?

BLANCHE I'm – not sure I did.

EUNICE Well, that's where she's at, watchin' her husband bowl.

[*There is a pause*] You want to leave your suitcase here an' go find her?

BLANCHE No.

NEGRO WOMAN I'll go tell her you come.

BLANCHE Thanks.

NEGRO WOMAN You welcome. [*She goes out.*]

EUNICE She wasn't expecting you?

BLANCHE No. No, not tonight.

EUNICE Well, why don't you just go in and make yourself at home till they get back.

BLANCHE How could I – do that?

EUNICE We own this place so I can let you in.

blind shutter, window shade (*Jalousie*)
dim out to become dim or almost dark

[*She gets up and opens the downstairs door. A light goes on behind the blind, turning it light blue. Blanche slowly follows her into the downstairs flat. The surrounding areas dim out as the interior is lighted.*]

[*Two rooms can be seen, not too clearly defined. The one first entered is primarily a kitchen but contains a folding bed to be used by Blanche. The room beyond this is a bedroom. Off this room is a narrow door to a bathroom.*]

defensive feeling under attack and, hence, quick to justify one's actions
messed up in disorder, not very tidy

EUNICE [*defensively, noticing Blanche's look*] It's sort of messed up right now but when it's clean it's real sweet.

BLANCHE Is it?

EUNICE Uh-huh, I think so. So you're Stella's sister?

BLANCHE Yes. [*Wanting to get rid of her*] Thanks for letting me in.

EUNICE *Por nada*, as the Mexicans say, *por nada!* Stella spoke of you.

BLANCHE Yes?

EUNICE I think she said you taught school.

BLANCHE Yes.

EUNICE And you're from Mississippi, huh?

BLANCHE Yes.

EUNICE She showed me a picture of your home-place, the plantation.

BLANCHE Belle Reve?

EUNICE A great big place with white columns.

BLANCHE Yes ...

EUNICE A place like that must be awful hard to keep up.

BLANCHE If you will excuse me, I'm just about to drop.

EUNICE Sure, honey. Why don't you set down?

BLANCHE What I meant was I'd like to be left alone.

EUNICE [*offended*] Aw. I'll make myself scarce, in that case.

BLANCHE I didn't mean to be rude, but –

EUNICE I'll drop by the bowling alley an' hustle her up.

[*She goes out the door.*]

[*Blanche sits in a chair very stiffly with her shoulders slightly hunched and her legs pressed close together and her hands tightly clutching her purse as if she were quite cold. After a while the blind look goes out of her eyes and she begins to look slowly around. A cat screeches. She catches her breath with a startled gesture. Suddenly she notices something in a half-opened closet. She springs up and crosses to it, and removes a whiskey bottle. She pours a half tumbler of whiskey and tosses it down. She carefully replaces the bottle and washes out the tumbler at the sink. Then she resumes her seat in front of the table.*]

BLANCHE [*faintly to herself*] I've got to keep hold of myself!

[*Stella comes quickly around the corner of the building and runs to the door of the downstairs flat.*]

STELLA [*calling out joyfully*] *Blanche!*

[*For a moment they stare at each other. Then Blanche springs up and runs to her with a wild cry.*]

BLANCHE Stella, oh, Stella, Stella! Stella for Star!

[*She begins to speak with feverish vivacity as if she feared for either of them to stop and think. They catch each other in a spasmodic embrace.*]

BLANCHE Now, then, let me look at you. But don't you look at me, Stella, no, no, no, not till later, not till I've bathed and rested! And turn that over-light off! Turn that off! I won't be looked at in this merciless glare! [*Stella laughs and complies*] Come back here now! Oh, my baby! Stella! Stella for

por nada (Spanish) that's okay

Belle Reve name of a typical Southern mansion (French, but it should correctly be "Beau Rêve; don't forget that Louisiana has been strongly influenced by French culture)

make oneself scarce (informal) to go away and stay away

hustle sb up (informal) to cause sb to do sth quickly, to hurry

hunched raised because you are tense or anxious (shoulders)
clutch to hold eagerly or tightly, to grasp
purse (AE) a woman's handbag (in GB, a purse is usually a small bag in which women keep paper money and coins, which is "a wallet" in America)
screech to howl, to yelp
startled suddenly surprised and shocked

Contrast the two sisters.

closet (AE) a cupboard for clothes, household supplies, etc. (in GB, it is called "a cupboard" or "a wardrobe")
tumbler an ordinary drinking glass without foot or stem
toss down (here) to drink quickly
vivacity [vɪˈvæsəti] liveliness, having a lot of energy and charm
spasmodic happening at irregular moments
over-light blinding ceiling light
comply (formal) to do what one is asked to do

Star! [*She embraces her again*] I thought you would never come back to this horrible place! What am I saying? I didn't mean to say that. I meant to be nice about it and say – Oh, what a convenient location and such – Haa-ha! Precious lamb! You haven't said a *word* to me.

STELLA You haven't given me a chance to, honey! [*She laughs, but her glance at Blanche is a little anxious.*]

BLANCHE Well, now you talk. Open your pretty mouth and talk while I look around for some liquor! I know you must have some liquor on the place! Where could it be, I wonder? Oh, I spy, I spy!

spy to see sth after looking for it (often used in children's games)

pant to breathe rapidly and heavily; to gasp, as from running

[*She rushes to the closet and removes the bottle; she is shaking all over and panting for breath as she tries to laugh. The bottle nearly slips from her grasp.*]

STELLA [*noticing*] Blanche, you sit down and let me pour the drinks. I don't know what we've got to mix with. Maybe a coke's in the icebox. Look'n see, honey, while I'm –

BLANCHE No coke, honey, not with my nerves tonight! Where – where – where is –?

STELLA Stanley? Bowling! He loves it. They're having a – found some soda! – tournament ...

BLANCHE Just water, baby, to chase it! Now don't get worried, your sister hasn't turned into a drunkard, she's just all shaken up and hot and tired and dirty! You sit down, now, and explain this place to me! What are you doing in a place like this?

STELLA Now, Blanche –

BLANCHE Oh, I'm not going to be hypocritical, I'm going to be honestly critical about it! Never, never, never in my worst dreams could I picture – Only Poe! Only Mr. Edgar Allan Poe! – could do it justice! Out there I suppose is the ghoul-haunted woodland of Weir! [*She laughs.*]

hypocritical [ˌhɪpəˈkrɪtɪkl] behaving differently from what one pretends to believe (*heuchlerisch*)

Poe the American poet, essayist and short story writer Edgar Allan Poe (1809–1849); the lines quoted are from his ballad "Ulalume" (1847)

ghoul-haunted [guːl] regularly visited by evil spirits and evil thoughts

Weir [wɪə] a name invented by Poe because he believed that the word had a haunting quality

STELLA No, honey, those are the L & N tracks.

BLANCHE No, now seriously, putting joking aside. Why didn't you tell me, why didn't you write me, honey, why didn't you let me know?

STELLA [*carefully, pouring herself a drink*] Tell you what, Blanche?

BLANCHE Why, that you had to live in these conditions!

STELLA Aren't you being a little intense about it? It's not that bad at all! New Orleans isn't like other cities.

intense having strong feelings and great seriousness about sth (used disapprovingly)

BLANCHE This has got nothing to do with New Orleans. You might as well say – forgive me, blessed baby! [*She suddenly stops short*] The subject is closed!

STELLA [*a little drily*] Thanks.

[*During the pause, Blanche stares at her. She smiles at Blanche.*]

BLANCHE [*looking down at her glass, which shakes in her hand*] You're all I've got in the world, and you're not glad to see me!

STELLA [*sincerely*] Why, Blanche, you know that's not true.

BLANCHE No? – I'd forgotten how quiet you were.

STELLA You never did give me a chance to say much, Blanche. So I just got in the habit of being quiet around you.

BLANCHE [*vaguely*] A good habit to get into ... [*then, abruptly*] You haven't asked me how I happened to get away from the school before the spring term ended.

STELLA Well, I thought you'd volunteer that information – if you wanted to tell me.

BLANCHE You thought I'd been fired?

STELLA No, I – thought you might have – resigned ...

BLANCHE I was so exhausted by all I'd been through my – nerves broke. [*Nervously tamping cigarette*] I was on the verge of – lunacy, almost! So Mr. Graves – Mr. Graves is the high school superintendent – he suggested I take a leave of absence. I couldn't put all of those details into the wire ... [*She drinks quickly*] Oh, this buzzes right through me and feels so *good!*

STELLA Won't you have another?

BLANCHE No, one's my limit.

STELLA Sure?

BLANCHE You haven't said a word about my appearance.

STELLA You look just fine.

BLANCHE God love you for a liar! Daylight never exposed so total a ruin! But you – you've put on some weight, yes, you're just as plump as a little partridge! And it's so becoming to you!

STELLA Now, Blanche –

BLANCHE Yes, it is, it is or I wouldn't say it! You just have to watch around the hips a little. Stand up.

STELLA Not now.

BLANCHE You hear me? I said stand up! [*Stella complies reluctantly*] You messy child, you, you've spilt something on the pretty white lace collar! About your hair – you ought to have it cut in a feather bob with your dainty features. Stella, you have a maid, don't you?

STELLA No. With only two rooms it's –

BLANCHE What? *Two* rooms, did you say?

STELLA This one and – [*She is embarrassed.*]

BLANCHE The other one? [*She laughs sharply. There is an embarrassed silence.*]

I am going to take just one little tiny nip more, sort of to put the stopper on, so to speak ... Then put the bottle away so I

volunteer to freely offer to do sth without being expressly asked

tamp press or push down
on the verge of at the point of, close to
lunacy ['luːnəsi] madness, craziness
superintendent sb who is in charge of all schools in an area
this buzzes right through me (slang) *das geht mir durch und durch*

partridge *Rebhuhn*
becoming making sb look attractive

reluctant [rɪ'lʌktənt] unwilling, disinclined, hesitating
cut in a feather bob (hair) cut short with curly strands of hair
dainty delicately pretty; lovely

nip small amount of alcoholic drink
put the stopper on (here) to have one last drink (a stopper is used to close a bottle)

won't be tempted. [*She rises*] I want you to look at *my* figure! [*She turns around*] You know I haven't put on one ounce in ten years, Stella? I weigh what I weighed the summer you left Belle Reve. The summer Dad died and you left us ...

STELLA [*a little wearily*] It's just incredible, Blanche, how well you're looking.

uncomfortable [ʌn'kʌmfətəbl] awkward, feeling embarrassed

BLANCHE: [*They both laugh uncomfortably*] But, Stella, there's only two rooms, I don't see where you're going to put me!

STELLA We're going to put you in here.

collapsible collapsible bed, *Klappbett*

BLANCHE What kind of bed's this – one of those collapsible things?

[*She sits on it.*]

STELLA Does it feel all right?

dubious ['dju:biəs] feeling doubt, sceptical
give (here) to be too soft

BLANCHE [*dubiously*] Wonderful, honey. I don't like a bed that gives much. But there's no door between the two rooms, and Stanley – will it be decent?

STELLA Stanley is Polish, you know.

BLANCHE Oh, yes. They're something like Irish, aren't they?

STELLA Well –

highbrow ['hɪbraʊ] intellectual
middlebrow sb not really interested in intellectual matters
lowbrow sb with virtually no intellectual tastes

BLANCHE Only not so – highbrow? [*They both laugh again in the same way.*] I brought some nice clothes to meet all your lovely friends in.

STELLA I'm afraid you won't think they are lovely.

BLANCHE What are they like?

STELLA They're Stanley's friends.

BLANCHE Polacks?

STELLA They're a mixed lot, Blanche.

heterogeneous [ˌhetərəʊ'dʒi:niəs] composed of unlike and dissimilar elements

BLANCHE Heterogeneous – types?

STELLA Oh, yes. Yes, types is right!

BLANCHE Well – anyhow – I brought nice clothes and I'll wear them. I guess you're hoping I'll say I'll put up at a hotel, but I'm not going to put up at a hotel. I want to be *near* you, got to be *with* somebody, I *can't* be *alone*! Because – as you must have noticed – I'm – *not* very *well* ... [*Her voice drops and her look is frightened.*]

overwrought [ˌəʊvə'rɔ:t] very nervous and excited because tired or fatigued

STELLA You seem a little bit nervous or overwrought or something.

BLANCHE Will Stanley like me, or will I just be a visiting in-law, Stella? I couldn't stand that.

STELLA You'll get along fine together, if you'll just try not to – well – compare him with men that we went out with at home.

BLANCHE Is he so – different?

STELLA Yes. A different species.

BLANCHE In what way; what's he like?

STELLA Oh, you can't describe someone you're in love with! Here's a picture of him! [*She hands a photograph to Blanche.*]

BLANCHE An officer?

STELLA A Master Sergeant in the Engineers' Corps. Those are decorations!

BLANCHE He had those on when you met him?

STELLA I assure you I wasn't just blinded by all the brass.

BLANCHE That's not what I –

STELLA But of course there were things to adjust myself to later on.

BLANCHE Such as his civilian background! [*Stella laughs uncertainly*] How did he take it when you said I was coming?

STELLA Oh, Stanley doesn't know yet.

BLANCHE [*frightened*] You – haven't told him?

STELLA He's on the road a good deal.

BLANCHE Oh. Travels?

STELLA Yes.

BLANCHE Good. I mean – isn't it?

STELLA [*half to herself*] I can hardly stand it when he is away for a night ...

BLANCHE Why, Stella!

STELLA When he's away for a week I nearly go wild!

BLANCHE Gracious!

STELLA And when he comes back I cry on his lap like a baby ... [*She smiles to herself.*]

BLANCHE I guess that is what is meant by being in love ... [*Stella looks up with a radiant smile.*] Stella –

STELLA What?

BLANCHE [*in an uneasy rush*] I haven't asked you the things you probably thought I was going to ask. And so I'll expect you to be understanding about what *I* have to tell you.

STELLA What, Blanche? [*Her face turns anxious.*]

BLANCHE Well, Stella – you're going to reproach me, I know that you're bound to reproach me – but before you do – take into consideration – you left! I stayed and struggled! You came to New Orleans and looked out for yourself. *I* stayed at *Belle Reve* and tried to hold it together! I'm not meaning this in any reproachful way, but *all* the burden descended on *my* shoulders.

STELLA The best I could do was make my own living, Blanche. [*Blanche begins to shake again with intensity.*]

BLANCHE I know, I know. But you are the one that abandoned Belle Reve, not I! I stayed and fought for it, bled for it, almost died for it!

Master Sergeant *Stabsfeldwebel* (military title)
Engineers' Corps *Pioniertruppe*
decoration a military medal as a special sign of honour
brass (here) medal, decoration (especially in the U.S.A., the word can also refer to the people who hold important positions)
adjust oneself to to become gradually familiar with a new situation, to conform

radiant (of a smile) showing pleasure or love

uneasy uncomfortable, not relaxed
rush a sudden strong feeling of excitement

reproach to accuse sb of a fault, to blame (cf. four lines further down: reproachful)

intensity great seriousness and strong emotion

A typical Southern Mansion

outburst a sudden release of feeling or energy

checked having a regular pattern of squares in different colours

you're a fine one *ausgerechnet du musst das sagen*

graveyard cemetery, churchyard

coffin box in which a dead body is buried

STELLA Stop this hysterical outburst and tell me what's happened! What do you mean fought and bled? What kind of –

BLANCHE I knew you would, Stella. I knew you would take this attitude about it!

STELLA About – what? – please!

BLANCHE [*slowly*] The loss – the loss ...

STELLA Belle Reve? Lost, is it? No!

BLANCHE Yes, Stella.

[*They stare at each other across the yellow-checked linoleum of the table. Blanche slowly nods her head and Stella looks slowly down at her hands folded on the table. The music of the "blue piano" grows louder. Blanche touches her handkerchief to her forehead.*]

STELLA But how did it go? What happened?

BLANCHE [*springing up*] You're a fine one to ask me how it went!

STELLA Blanche!

BLANCHE You're a fine one to sit there accusing me of it!

STELLA *Blanche!*

BLANCHE I, I, *I* took the blows in my face and my body! All of those deaths! The long parade to the graveyard! Father, mother! Margaret, that dreadful way! So big with it, it couldn't be put in a coffin! But had to be burned like rubbish! You just came home in time for the funerals, Stella.

And funerals are pretty compared to deaths. Funerals are quiet, but deaths – not always. Sometimes their breathing is hoarse, and sometimes it rattles, and sometimes they even cry out to you, "Don't let me go!" Even the old, sometimes, say, "Don't let me go." As if you were able to stop them! But funerals are quiet, with pretty flowers. And, oh, what gorgeous boxes they pack them away in! Unless you were there at the bed when they cried out, "Hold me!" you'd never suspect there was the struggle for breath and bleeding. You didn't dream, but I saw! *Saw! Saw!* And now you sit there telling me with your eyes that I let the place go! How in hell do you think all that sickness and dying was paid for? Death is expensive, Miss Stella! And old Cousin Jessie's right after Margaret's, hers! Why, the Grim Reaper had put up his tent on our doorstep! ... Stella. Belle Reve was his headquarters! Honey – that's how it slipped through my fingers! Which of them left us a fortune? Which of them left a cent of insurance even? Only poor Jessie – one hundred to pay for her coffin. That was all, Stella! And I with my pitiful salary at the school. Yes, accuse me! Sit there and stare at me, thinking I let the place go! *I* let the place go? Where were *you*! In bed with your – Polack!

STELLA [*springing*] Blanche! You be still! That's enough! [*She starts out.*]

BLANCHE Where are you going?

STELLA I'm going into the bathroom to wash my face.

BLANCHE Oh, Stella, Stella, you're crying!

STELLA Does that surprise you?

BLANCHE Forgive me – I didn't mean to –

[*The sound of men's voices is heard. Stella goes into the bathroom, closing the door behind her. When the men appear, and Blanche realizes it must be Stanley returning, she moves uncertainly from the bathroom door to the dressing table, looking apprehensively toward the front door. Stanley enters, followed by Steve and Mitch. Stanley pauses near his door, Steve by the foot of the spiral stair, and Mitch is slightly above and to the right of them, about to go out. As the men enter, we hear some of the following dialogue.*]

STANLEY Is that how he got it?

STEVE Sure that's how he got it. He hit the old weather-bird for 300 bucks on a six-number-ticket.

MITCH Don't tell him those things; he'll believe it.

[*Mitch starts out.*]

STANLEY [*restraining Mitch*] Hey, Mitch – come back here.

[*Blanche, at the sound of voices, retires in the bedroom. She picks up Stanley's photo from dressing table, looks at it, puts it*

hoarse harsh and grating in sound, rough

gorgeous ['gɔːdʒəs] beautiful, magnificent

the Grim Reaper (here) Death (cf. *der grimmige Schnitter*)

apprehensive anxious, fearful and uneasy

buck (informal) dollar, cf. AE
grand a thousand dollars
dime ten cents
nickel five cents

dart to move suddenly and fast

Jax beer Mexican beer (brand name)

What do the stage directions say about Stanley? Think of possible conflicts emerging from a situation that has Stanley, Stella and Blanche living in close quarters.

screen door outer door consisting of a frame covered with mesh to keep insects out
compact solid and strong
implicit understood without being openly stated or plainly apparent
indulgence giving oneself up to the gratification of one's wishes, satisfying one's desires
auxiliary [ɔːg'zɪliəri] giving help and assistance
appreciation [əˌpriːʃi'eɪʃn] enjoyment because one understands and esteems s. th.
gaudy bright and showy in a cheap way, lacking in good taste
seed-bearer (here) a reference to his pride in his manliness (*Samenträger*)
size up to look at sb or sth and make a judgement about them
crude vulgar, coarse, lacking in tact or taste, rude, especially in a sexual way
Laurel a town in Mississippi, about 140 miles northeast of New Orleans

down. When Stanley enters the apartment, she darts and hides behind the screen at the head of bed.]

STEVE [*to Stanley and Mitch*] Hey, are we playin' poker tomorrow?

STANLEY Sure – at Mitch's.

MITCH [*hearing this, returns quickly to the stair rail*] No – not at my place. My mother's still sick!

STANLEY Okay, at my place ... [*Mitch starts out again*] But you bring the beer!

[*Mitch pretends not to hear, – calls out "Goodnight all," and goes out, singing.*]

EUNICE [*heard from above*] Break it up down there! I made the spaghetti dish and ate it myself.

STEVE [*going upstairs*] I told you and phoned you we was playing. [*To the men*] Jax beer!

EUNICE You never phoned me once.

STEVE I told you at breakfast – and phoned you at lunch ...

EUNICE Well, never mind about that. You just get yourself home here once in a while.

STEVE You want it in the papers?

[*More laughter and shouts of parting come from the men. Stanley throws the screen door of the kitchen open and comes in. He is of medium height, about five feet eight or nine, and strongly, compactly built. Animal joy in his being is implicit in all his movements and attitudes. Since earliest manhood the center of his life has been pleasure with women, the giving and taking of it, not with weak indulgence, dependently, but with the power and pride of a richly feathered male bird among hens. Branching out from this complete and satisfying center are all the auxiliary channels of his life, such as his heartiness with men, his appreciation of rough humor, his love of good drink and food and games, his car, his radio, everything that is his, that bears his emblem of the gaudy seed-bearer. He sizes women up at a glance, with sexual classifications, crude images flashing into his mind and determining the way he smiles at them.*]

BLANCHE [*drawing involuntarily back from his stare*] You must be Stanley. I'm Blanche.

STANLEY Stella's sister?

BLANCHE Yes.

STANLEY H'lo. Where's the little woman?

BLANCHE In the bathroom.

STANLEY Oh. Didn't know you were coming in town.

BLANCHE I – uh –

STANLEY Where you from, Blanche?

BLANCHE Why, I – live in Laurel.

[*He has crossed to the closet and removed the whiskey bottle.*]

STANLEY In Laurel, huh? Oh, yeah. Yeah, in Laurel, that's right. Not in my territory. Liquor goes fast in hot weather. [*He holds the bottle to the light to observe its depletion.*] Have a shot?

BLANCHE No, I – rarely touch it.

STANLEY Some people rarely touch it, but it touches them often.

BLANCHE [*faintly*] Ha-ha.

STANLEY My clothes 're stickin' to me. Do you mind if I make myself comfortable? [*He starts to remove his shirt.*]

BLANCHE Please, please do.

STANLEY Be comfortable is my motto.

BLANCHE It's mine, too. It's hard to stay looking fresh. I haven't washed or even powdered my face and – here you are!

STANLEY You know you can catch cold sitting around in damp things, especially when you been exercising hard like bowling is. You're a teacher, aren't you?

BLANCHE Yes.

STANLEY What do you teach, Blanche?

BLANCHE English.

STANLEY I never was a very good English student. How long you here for, Blanche?

BLANCHE I – don't know yet.

STANLEY You going to shack up here?

BLANCHE I thought I would if it's not inconvenient for you all.

STANLEY Good.

BLANCHE Traveling wears me out.

STANLEY Well, take it easy.

[*A cat screeches near the window. Blanche springs up.*]

BLANCHE What's that?

STANLEY Cats ... Hey, Stella!

STELLA [*faintly, from the bathroom*] Yes, Stanley.

STANLEY Haven't fallen in, have you? [*He grins at Blanche. She tries unsuccessfully to smile back. There is a silence*] I'm afraid I'll strike you as being the unrefined type. Stella's spoke of you a good deal. You were married once, weren't you?

[*The music of the polka rises up, faint in the distance.*]

BLANCHE Yes. When I was quite young.

STANLEY What happened?

BLANCHE The boy – the boy died. [*She sinks back down*] I'm afraid I'm – going to be sick!

[*Her head falls on her arms.*]

depletion [dɪ'pli:ʃn] being partly emptied
shot (AE) a drink of liquor

shack up (slang) to live in a certain room for a while
inconvenient [ˌɪnkən'vi:niənt] causing problems for sb

unrefined (formal) uncultured, not very well educated

Compare the register Blanche uses with that of the other characters, especially Stanley. What does the use of language indicate?

Scene Two

It is six o'clock the following evening. Blanche is bathing. Stella is completing her toilette. Blanche's dress, a flowered print, is laid out on Stella's bed. Stanley enters the kitchen from outside, leaving the door open on the perpetual "blue piano" around the corner.

perpetual [pəˈpetʃuəl] repeated many times, seemingly unending (often annoying)

Stanley and Stella's house in New Orleans, from Elia Kazan's film

STANLEY What's all this monkey doings?

STELLA Oh, Stan! [*She jumps up and kisses him which he accepts with lordly composure*] I'm taking Blanche to Galatoire's for supper and then to a show, because it's your poker night.

STANLEY How about my supper, huh? I'm not going to no Galatoire's for supper!

STELLA I put you a cold plate on ice.

STANLEY Well, isn't that just dandy!

STELLA I'm going to try to keep Blanche out till the party breaks up because I don't know how she would take it. So we'll go to one of the little places in the Quarter afterwards and you'd better give me some money.

STANLEY Where is she?

STELLA She's soaking in a hot tub to quiet her nerves. She's terribly upset.

STANLEY Over what?

STELLA She's been through such an ordeal.

STANLEY Yeah?

STELLA Stan, we've – lost Belle Reve!

STANLEY The place in the country?

What's all this monkey doings? (slang) *Was soll das alles? Wozu der ganze Quatsch?*
composure [kəmˈpəʊʒə] state of being calm and unmoved
Galatoire's name of a French restaurant in the Vieux Carré

cold plate plate of cold cuts (thinly cut pieces of cooked meat eaten cold)
dandy (informal) fine, first-rate

Quarter the French Quarter, the Vieux Carré

soak in a hot tub to spend a long time taking a bath (tub: *Badewanne*)

ordeal [ɔːˈdiːl] a difficult, painful, and trying experience

STELLA Yes.

STANLEY How?

STELLA [*vaguely*] Oh, it had to be – sacrificed or something. [*There is a pause while Stanley considers. Stella is changing into her dress*] When she comes in be sure to say something nice about her appearance. And, oh! Don't mention the baby. I haven't said anything yet, I'm waiting until she gets in a quieter condition.

STANLEY [*ominously*] So?

STELLA And try to understand her and be nice to her, Stan.

BLANCHE [*singing in the bathroom*] "From the land of the sky blue water, They brought a captive maid!"

STELLA She wasn't expecting to find us in such a small place. You see I'd tried to gloss things over a little in my letters.

STANLEY So?

STELLA And admire her dress and tell her she's looking wonderful. That's important with Blanche. Her little weakness!

STANLEY Yeah. I get the idea. Now let's skip back a little to where you said the country place was disposed of.

STELLA Oh! – yes ...

STANLEY How about that? Let's have a few more details on that subjeck.

STELLA It's best not to talk much about it until she's calmed down.

STANLEY So that's the deal, huh? Sister Blanche cannot be annoyed with business details right now!

STELLA You saw how she was last night.

STANLEY Uh-hum, I saw how she was. Now let's have a gander at the bill of sale.

STELLA I haven't seen any.

STANLEY She didn't show you no papers, no deed of sale or nothing like that, huh?

STELLA It seems like it wasn't sold.

STANLEY Well, what in hell was it then, give away? To charity?

STELLA Shhh! She'll hear you.

STANLEY I don't care if she hears me. Let's see the papers!

STELLA There weren't any papers, she didn't show any papers, I don't care about papers.

STANLEY Have you ever heard of the Napoleonic code?

STELLA No, Stanley, I haven't heard of the Napoleonic code and if I have, I don't see what it –

STANLEY Let me enlighten you on a point or two, baby.

STELLA Yes?

STANLEY In the state of Louisiana we have the Napoleonic code according to which what belongs to the wife belongs to the

ominous making sb feel that sth bad is going to happen; threatening

captive taken or held prisoner; the lines Blanche is singing are from a popular ballad written by N.R. Eberhart (1871–1944)

➔ Stanley answers "so" to Stella's explanation of the loss of Belle Reve. How could the actor playing Stanley utter this monosyllable? What about his posture and facial expression at this moment?

gloss over to cover up; to make appear better than it is
skip back (here) to get back to a subject
dispose of to give away or sell; to get rid of
so that's the deal (informal) *so sieht das also aus*
have a gander at (also, take a gander at: slang) have a look at
bill of sale a written document showing that sb has sold or bought sth (*Verkaufsvertrag*)
deed of sale an official paper that is an agreement concerning who owns property (*Übertragungsurkunde*)

the Napoleonic code [nəˌpəʊli'ɒnik] Code Napoleon (body of French civil law enacted in 1804; model for the civil codes of many nations)
enlighten (formal) (sb on sth) to explain, to inform

husband and vice versa. For instance if I had a piece of property, or you had a piece of property –

Stella My head is swimming!

Stanley All right. I'll wait till she gets through soaking in a hot tub and then I'll inquire if *she* is acquainted with the Napoleonic code. It looks to me like you have been swindled, baby, and when you're swindled under the Napoleonic code I'm swindled *too.* And I don't like to be *swindled.*

Stella There's plenty of time to ask her questions later but if you do now she'll go to pieces again. I don't understand what happened to Belle Reve but you don't know how ridiculous you are being when you suggest that my sister or I or anyone of our family could have perpetrated a swindle on anyone else.

Stanley Then where's the money if the place was sold?

Stella Not sold – *lost, lost!*

[*He stalks into bedroom, and she follows him.*]

Stanley!

[*He pulls open the wardrobe trunk standing in middle of room and jerks out an armful of dresses.*]

Stanley Open your eyes to this stuff! You think she got them out of a teacher's pay?

Stella Hush!

Stanley Look at these feathers and furs that she come here to preen herself in! What's this here? A solid-gold dress, I believe! And this one! What is these here? Fox-pieces! [*He blows on them*] Genuine fox fur-pieces, a half a mile long! Where are your fox-pieces, Stella? Bushy snow-white ones, no less! Where are your white fox-pieces?

Stella Those are inexpensive summer furs that Blanche has had a long time.

Stanley I got an acquaintance who deals in this sort of merchandise. I'll have him in here to appraise it. I'm willing to bet you there's thousands of dollars invested in this stuff here!

Stella Don't be such an idiot, Stanley!

[*He hurls the furs on the daybed. Then he jerks open small drawer in the trunk and pulls up a fist-full of costume jewelry.*]

Stanley And what have we here? The treasure chest of a pirate!

Stella Oh, Stanley!

Stanley Pearls! Ropes of them! What is this sister of yours, a deep-sea diver? Bracelets of solid gold, too! Where are your pearls and gold bracelets?

Stella Shhh! Be still, Stanley!

vice versa [ˌvaɪsəˈvɜːsə] or [ˌvaɪsˈvɜːsə] used to say that the opposite of what you have said is equally true; conversely

go to pieces to be so upset that you can no longer act normally

perpetrate (formal) to commit (a crime), to do sth that is wrong

wardrobe trunk a large trunk for carrying clothes

jerk out to pull out suddenly and roughly

preen oneself to dress oneself up (like a bird trimming its feathers)

merchandise goods, things bought and sold

appraise to judge the quality of; to set a prize for; to decide the value of sth officially

daybed a couch that can also be used as a bed

costume jewellery cheap jewellery set with imitation gems

bracelet an ornamental band or chain worn about the wrist or arm

STANLEY And diamonds! A crown for an empress!

STELLA A rhinestone tiara she wore to a costume ball.

STANLEY What's rhinestone?

STELLA Next door to glass.

STANLEY Are you kidding? I have an acquaintance that works in a jewelry store. I'll have him in here to make an appraisal of this. Here's your plantation, or what was left of it, here!

STELLA You have no idea how stupid and horrid you're being! Now close that trunk before she comes out of the bathroom!

[*He kicks the trunk partly closed and sits on the kitchen table.*]

STANLEY The Kowalskis and the DuBois have different notions.

STELLA [*angrily*] Indeed they have, thank heavens! – *I'm* going outside.

[*She snatches up her white hat and gloves and crosses to the outside door.*] You come out with me while Blanche is getting dressed.

STANLEY Since when do you give me orders?

STELLA Are you going to stay here and insult her?

STANLEY You're damn tootin' I'm going to stay here.

[*Stella goes out to the porch. Blanche comes out of the bathroom in a red satin robe.*]

BLANCHE [*airily*] Hello, Stanley! Here I am, all freshly bathed and scented, and feeling like a brand new human being!

[*He lights a cigarette.*]

STANLEY That's good.

BLANCHE [*drawing the curtains at the windows*] Excuse me while I slip on my pretty new dress!

STANLEY Go right ahead, Blanche.

[*She closes the drapes between the rooms.*]

BLANCHE I understand there's to be a little card party to which we ladies are cordially *not* invited!

STANLEY [*ominously*] Yeah?

[*Blanche throws off her robe and slips into a flowered print dress.*]

BLANCHE Where's Stella?

STANLEY Out on the porch.

BLANCHE I'm going to ask a favor of you in a moment.

STANLEY What could that be, I wonder?

BLANCHE Some buttons in back! You may enter!

[*He crosses through drapes with a smoldering look.*]

How do I look?

STANLEY You look all right.

BLANCHE Many thanks! Now the buttons!

STANLEY I can't do nothing with them.

---

rhinestone an artificial gem made of hard glass that is intended to look like a diamond
tiara [ti'ɑːrə] a piece of jewellery like a small crown (a woman's crownlike headdress)
Are you kidding? (slang) *Du machst wohl Witze.*
appraisal the action of judging the quality of sth

➔ How do the Kowalskis and the DuBois differ? Make a list of their differences and expand that list as you read on.

you're damm tootin' (slang) *darauf kannst du dich verlassen*

robe (AE) bathrobe, dressing gown
airy affectedly light-hearted
scented with a pleasant smell, perfumed

drapes (AE, pl.) long heavy curtains

cordial friendly in a polite and formal way

print dress a dress or blouse made of cloth printed with a design

smoldering showing suppressed anger or hate (to smoulder: to burn and smoke without flame)

drag breath of smoke from a cigarette

raid a sudden attack or invasion
stylish smart, fashionable

doll (slang) an attractive woman (a doll is a child's toy)

that shut her up like a clam that stopped her talking (clam: *Muschel*)

take sb in to cheat, to trick, to deceive

cast a spell over to attract sb strongly and keep their attention (a spell: magic words)

let's cut the re-bop (AE, slang) *hör jetzt mit dem Mist auf* (re-bop or bebop or bop: a style of jazz depending on strong rhythm and seemingly nonsensical words which are sung to it)

BLANCHE You men with your big clumsy fingers. May I have a drag on your cig?

STANLEY Have one for yourself.

BLANCHE Why, thanks! ... It looks like my trunk has exploded.

STANLEY Me an' Stella were helping you unpack.

BLANCHE Well, you certainly did a fast and thorough job of it!

STANLEY It looks like you raided some stylish shops in Paris.

BLANCHE Ha-ha! Yes – clothes are my passion!

STANLEY What does it cost for a string of fur-pieces like that?

BLANCHE Why, those were a tribute from an admirer of mine!

STANLEY He must have had a lot of – admiration!

BLANCHE Oh, in my youth I excited some admiration. But look at me now! [*She smiles at him radiantly*] Would you think it possible that I was once considered to be – attractive?

STANLEY Your looks are okay.

BLANCHE I was fishing for a compliment, Stanley.

STANLEY I don't go in for that stuff.

BLANCHE What – stuff?

STANLEY Compliments to women about their looks. I never met a woman that didn't know if she was good-looking or not without being told, and some of them give themselves credit for more than they've got. I once went out with a doll who said to me, "I am the glamorous type, I am the glamorous type!" I said, "So what?"

BLANCHE And what did she say then?

STANLEY She didn't say nothing. That shut her up like a clam.

BLANCHE Did it end the romance?

STANLEY It ended the conversation – that was all. Some men are took in by this Hollywood glamor stuff and some men are not.

BLANCHE I'm sure you belong in the second category.

STANLEY That's right.

BLANCHE I cannot imagine any witch of a woman casting a spell over you.

STANLEY That's – right.

BLANCHE You're simple, straightforward and honest, a little bit on the primitive side I should think. To interest you a woman would have to – [*She pauses with an indefinite gesture.*]

STANLEY [*slowly*] Lay ... her cards on the table.

BLANCHE [*smiling*] Well, I never cared for wishy-washy people. That was why, when you walked in here last night, I said to myself – "My sister has married a man!" – Of course that was all that I could tell about you.

STANLEY [*booming*] Now let's cut the re-bop!

BLANCHE [*pressing hands to her ears*] Ouuuuu!

Stella [*calling from the steps]* Stanley! You come out here and let Blanche finish dressing!

Blanche I'm through dressing, honey.

Stella Well, you come out, then.

Stanley Your sister and I are having a little talk.

Blanche [*lightly*] Honey, do me a favor. Run to the drug-store and get me a lemon-coke with plenty of chipped ice in it! – Will you do that for me, Sweetie?

Stella [*uncertainly*] Yes. [*She goes around the corner of the building.*]

Blanche The poor little thing was out there listening to us, and I have an idea she doesn't understand you as well as I do. ... All right; now, Mr. Kowalski, let us proceed without any more double-talk. I'm ready to answer all questions. I've nothing to hide. What is it?

Stanley There is such a thing in this State of Louisiana as the Napoleonic code, according to which whatever belongs to my wife is also mine – and vice versa.

Blanche My, but you have an impressive judicial air!

[*She sprays herself with her atomizer; then playfully sprays him with it. He seizes the atomizer and slams it down on the dresser. She throws back her head and laughs.*]

Stanley If I didn't know that you was my wife's sister I'd get ideas about you!

Blanche Such as what!

Stanley Don't play so dumb. You know what!

Blanche [*she puts the atomizer on the table*] All right. Cards on the table. That suits me. [*She turns to Stanley.*] I know I fib a good deal. After all, a woman's charm is fifty percent illusion, but when a thing is important I tell the truth, and this is the truth: I haven't cheated my sister or you or anyone else as long as I have lived.

Stanley Where's the papers? In the trunk?

Blanche Everything that I own is in that trunk.

[*Stanley crosses to the trunk, shoves it roughly open and begins to open compartments.*]

Blanche What in the name of heaven are you thinking of! What's in the back of that little boy's mind of yours? That I am absconding with something, attempting some kind of treachery on my sister? – Let me do that! It will be faster and simpler ... [*She crosses to the trunk and takes out a box*] I keep my papers mostly in this tin box. [*She opens it.*]

Stanley What's them underneath? [*He indicates another sheaf of paper.*]

Blanche These are love-letters, yellowing with antiquity, all

drug-store (AE) a shop where you can buy medicine or beauty products and, often, other merchandise as well (BE: pharmacy, chemist)
chip to cut or break into small pieces

double-talk deliberately confusing talk intended to deceive people

judicial [dʒu'dɪʃl] like a judge

Why does she spray him? What does this action tell you about Blanche in the light of the ongoing conversation? How does Stanley understand the action?

atomizer a container from which you can spray perfume
dresser (AE) a piece of furniture with a mirror on top
dumb [dʌm] (AE) stupid, silly
fib to tell a small or trivial lie

compartment a smaller enclosed place inside a larger place

abscond (formal) to run away and hide
treachery ['tretʃəri] disloyal action against sb who trusts you, betrayal of faith
sheaf a bundle (of papers)

fierce wild, violent, uncontrolled

don't pull that stuff (slang) *komm mir nicht mit solchem Quatsch*

cascade [kæs'keɪd] to fall or drop in a cascade (a small waterfall)

baffled confused, puzzled, failing to understand

vulnerable ['vʌlnərəbl] easily hurt

exhaustion [ɪg'zɔːstʃən] state of great weariness, of being completely used up

strong box a box or safe for storing valuables

mortgage ['mɔːgɪdʒ] the pledging of property to a creditor as security for the payment of a debt

improvident lacking foresight, failing to provide for the future

fornication sexual intercourse with sb you are not married to

verify confirm, state that sth is true or correct

acre ['eɪkə] a unit for measuring an area (4047 square metres)

endow (formal) to provide with, to give

peruse [pə'ruːz] (formal) to read carefully

from one boy. [*He snatches them up. She speaks fiercely*] Give those back to me!

STANLEY I'll have a look at them first!

BLANCHE The touch of your hands insults them!

STANLEY Don't pull that stuff!

[*He rips off the ribbon and starts to examine them. Blanche snatches them from him, and they cascade to the floor.*]

BLANCHE Now that you've touched them I'll burn them!

STANLEY [*staring, baffled*] What in hell are they?

BLANCHE [*on the floor gathering them up*] Poems a dead boy wrote. I hurt him the way that you would like to hurt me, but you can't! I'm not young and vulnerable any more. But my young husband was and I – never mind about that! Just give them back to me!

STANLEY What do you mean by saying you'll have to burn them?

BLANCHE I'm sorry, I must have lost my head for a moment. Everyone has something he won't let others touch because of their – intimate nature ...

[*She now seems faint with exhaustion and she sits down with the strong box and puts on a pair of glasses and goes methodically through a large stack of papers.*]

Ambler & Ambler. Hmmmmm ... Crabtree ... More Ambler & Ambler.

STANLEY What is Ambler & Ambler?

BLANCHE A firm that made loans on the place.

STANLEY Then it *was* lost on a mortgage?

BLANCHE [*touching her forehead*] That must've been what happened.

STANLEY I don't want no ifs, ands or buts! What's all the rest of them papers?

[*She hands him the entire box. He carries it to the table and starts to examine the papers.*]

BLANCHE [*picking up a large envelope containing more papers*] There are thousands of papers, stretching back over hundreds of years, affecting Belle Reve as, piece by piece, our improvident grandfathers and father and uncles and brothers exchanged the land for their epic fornications – to put it plainly! [*She removes her glasses with an exhausted laugh*] The four-letter word deprived us of our plantation, till finally all that was left – and Stella can verify that! – was the house itself and about twenty acres of ground, including a graveyard, to which now all but Stella and I have retreated. [*She pours the contents of the envelope on the table*] Here all of them are, all papers! I hereby endow you with them! Take

them, peruse them – commit them to memory, even! I think it's wonderfully fitting that Belle Reve should finally be this bunch of old papers in your big, capable hands! ... I wonder if Stella's come back with my lemon-coke ...
[*She leans back and closes her eyes.*]

STANLEY I have a lawyer acquaintance who will study these out.

BLANCHE Present them to him with a box of aspirin tablets.

STANLEY [*becoming somewhat sheepish*] You see, under the Napoleonic code – a man has to take an interest in his wife's affairs – especially now that she's going to have a baby.
[*Blanche opens her eyes. The "blue piano" sounds louder.*]

BLANCHE Stella? Stella going to have a baby? [*dreamily*] I didn't know she was going to have a baby!
[*She gets up and crosses to the outside door. Stella appears around the corner with a carton from the drugstore.*
Stanley goes into the bedroom with the envelope and the box.
The inner rooms fade to darkness and the outside wall of the house is visible. Blanche meets Stella at the foot of the steps to the sidewalk.]

BLANCHE Stella, Stella for star! How lovely to have a baby! It's all right. Everything's all right.

STELLA I'm sorry he did that to you.

BLANCHE Oh, I guess he's just not the type that goes for jasmine perfume, but maybe he's what we need to mix with our blood now that we've lost Belle Reve. We thrashed it out. I feel a bit shaky, but I think I handled it nicely, I laughed and treated it all as a joke. [*Steve and Pablo appear, carrying a case of beer.*] I called him a little boy and laughed and flirted. Yes, I was flirting with your husband! [*as the men approach*] The guests are gathering for the poker party. [*The two men pass between them, and enter the house.*] Which way do we go now, Stella – this way?

STELLA No, this way. [*She leads Blanche away.*]

BLANCHE [*laughing*] The blind are leading the blind!
[*A tamale vendor is heard calling.*]

VENDOR'S VOICE Red-hot!

sheepish uncomfortable and embarrassed because you know that you have done sth wrong

sidewalk (AE) the hard surface at the side of a street (BE: pavement)

Comment on Blanche's words. To what extent are they an implicit statement on the past and what prospect do they seem to hold out for the future?

jasmine ['dʒæzmɪn] *Jasmin*
thrash it out (informal) to discuss thoroughly to reach an agreement

tamale [tə'mɑ:li] native Mexican food of minced meat, tomato sauce and red pepper rolled in cornleaf, wrapped in corn husks
vendor sb who sells things (on the streets etc.)

Scene Three

THE POKER NIGHT.

Vincent van Gogh, The Night Café (1888)

lurid vivid in a harsh or shocking way; too brightly coloured
nocturnal (formal) of the night, happening at night
spectrum complete range of (colours, sound waves, opinions, etc.)
solid blue uniformly blue, nothing but blue
purple a blend or mixture of the colours blue and red
coarse not fine or delicate in form and texture
primary colors one of the three colours red, yellow or blue, which can be mixed to make any of the other colours
portiere a curtain, usually heavy, hung in a doorway
absorbed (of light or noise) taken in, sucked up
wild (in card games like poker) having any value specified by the owner
jack (card games) knave; *Bube* (one-eyed jacks: *Herzbube oder Pikbube)*

There is a picture of Van Gogh's of a billiard-parlor at night. The kitchen now suggests that sort of lurid nocturnal brilliance, the raw colors of childhood's spectrum. Over the yellow linoleum of the kitchen table hangs an electric bulb with a vivid green glass shade. The poker players – Stanley, Steve, Mitch and Pablo – wear colored shirts, solid blues, a purple, a red-and-white check, a light green, and they are men at the peak of their physical manhood, as coarse and direct and powerful as the primary colors. There are vivid slices of watermelon on the table, whiskey bottles and glasses. The bedroom is relatively dim with only the light that spills between the portieres and through the wide window on the street.

For a moment, there is absorbed silence as a hand is dealt.

STEVE Anything wild this deal?

PABLO One-eyed jacks are wild.

STEVE Give me two cards.

PABLO You, Mitch?

MITCH I'm out.

PABLO One.

MITCH Anyone want a shot?

STANLEY Yeah. Me.

PABLO Why don't somebody go to the Chinaman's and bring back a load of chop suey?

STANLEY When I'm losing you want to eat! Ante up! Openers? Openers! Get y'r ass off the table, Mitch. Nothing belongs on a poker table but cards, chips and whiskey.

[*He lurches up and tosses some watermelon rinds to the floor.*]

MITCH Kind of on your high horse, ain't you?

STANLEY How many?

STEVE Give me three.

STANLEY One.

MITCH I'm out again. I oughta go home pretty soon.

STANLEY Shut up.

MITCH I gotta sick mother. She don't go to sleep until I come in at night.

STANLEY Then why don't you stay home with her?

MITCH She says to go out, so I go, but I don't enjoy it. All the while I keep wondering how she is.

STANLEY Aw, for the sake of Jesus, go home, then!

PABLO What've you got?

STANLEY Spade flush.

MITCH You all are married. But I'll be alone when she goes. – I'm going to the bathroom.

STANLEY Hurry back and w'll fix you a sugar-tit.

MITCH Aw, go rut. [*He crosses through the bedroom into the bathroom.*]

STEVE [*dealing a hand*] Seven card stud. [*Telling his joke as he deals*] This ole farmer is out in back of his house sittin' down th'owing corn to the chickens when all at once he hears a loud cackle and this young hen comes lickety split around the side of the house with the rooster right behind her and gaining on her fast.

STANLEY [*impatient with the story*] Deal!

STEVE But when the rooster catches sight of the farmer th'owing the corn he puts on the brakes and lets the hen get away and starts pecking corn. And the old farmer says, "Lord God, I hopes I never gits *that* hongry!"

[*Steve and Pablo laugh. The sisters appear around the corner of the building.*]

STELLA The game is still going on.

BLANCHE How do I look?

STELLA Lovely, Blanche.

BLANCHE I feel so hot and frazzled. Wait till I powder before you open the door. Do I look done in?

STELLA Why no. You are as fresh as a daisy.

BLANCHE One that's been picked a few days.

---

ante up ['ænti] (card games) pay an amount of money (stake) into the pot to be able to take part in the game
lurch up to stand up in an uncontrolled, unsteady way
rind [raɪnd] the outer skin of a fruit
on one's high horse *auf dem hohen Roß* (feeling superior)

➋ What impression of Mitch do we get through the dialogue?

spade flush (poker) a hand of five spades (in the same suit), **spade** *Pik*, **clubs** *Kreuz*, **hearts** *Herz*, **diamonds** *Karo*

sugar-tit (slang; here) a sexy woman (a sugar-tit is a sugar-sweet pacifier for a baby in AE)
seven card stud (card game) a variety of poker

cackle loud sound made by chickens
lickety split (AE; informal) at great speed
rooster a male chicken (BE: cock)

peck (bird) pick up with its beak

frazzled (informal) physically or emotionally exhausted (very tired)
done in (informal) very tired
fresh as a daisy not tired and ready to do things (daisy: *Gänseblümchen*)

How is the idea created that the two women gatecrash an all-male party?

kibitz (informal) to be an onlooker (kibitzer) at a card game, especially one who volunteers advice

call it quits (informal) to stop doing sth

scrape to make a noise by rubbing roughly against a surface

whack (informal) hitting sth hard

[*Stella opens the door and they enter.*]

STELLA Well, well, well. I see you boys are still at it!

STANLEY Where you been?

STELLA Blanche and I took in a show. Blanche, this is Mr. Gonzales and Mr. Hubbell.

BLANCHE Please don't get up.

STANLEY Nobody's going to get up, so don't be worried.

STELLA How much longer is this game going to continue?

STANLEY Till we get ready to quit.

BLANCHE Poker is so fascinating. Could I kibitz?

STANLEY You could not. Why don't you women go up and sit with Eunice?

STELLA Because it is nearly two-thirty. [*Blanche crosses into the bedroom and partially closes the portieres*] Couldn't you call it quits after one more hand?

[*A chair scrapes. Stanley gives a loud whack of his hand on her thigh.*]

STELLA [*sharply*] That's not fun, Stanley.

[*The men laugh. Stella goes into the bedroom.*]

Thomas Hart Benton, Poker Night (1948)

STELLA It makes me so mad when he does that in front of people.

BLANCHE I think I will bathe.

STELLA Again?

BLANCHE My nerves are in knots. Is the bathroom occupied?

STELLA I don't know.

[*Blanche knocks. Mitch opens the door and comes out, still wiping his hands on a towel.*]

BLANCHE Oh! – good evening.

MITCH Hello. [*He stares at her.*]

STELLA Blanche, this is Harold Mitchell. My sister, Blanche DuBois.

MITCH [*with awkward courtesy*] How do you do, Miss DuBois?

STELLA How is your mother now, Mitch?

MITCH About the same, thanks. She appreciated your sending over that custard. – Excuse me, please.

[*He crosses slowly back into the kitchen, glancing back at Blanche and coughing a little shyly. He realizes he still has the towel in his hands and with an embarrassed laugh hands it to Stella. Blanche looks after him with a certain interest.*]

BLANCHE That one seems – superior to the others.

STELLA Yes, he is.

BLANCHE I thought he had a sort of sensitive look.

STELLA His mother is sick.

BLANCHE Is he married?

STELLA No.

BLANCHE Is he a wolf?

STELLA Why, Blanche! [*Blanche laughs.*] I don't think he would be.

BLANCHE What does – what does he do?

[*She is unbuttoning her blouse.*]

STELLA He's on the precision bench in the spare parts department at the plant Stanley travels for.

BLANCHE Is that something much?

STELLA No. Stanley's the only one of his crowd that's likely to get anywhere.

BLANCHE What makes you think Stanley will?

STELLA Look at him.

BLANCHE I've looked at him.

STELLA Then you should know.

BLANCHE I'm sorry, but I haven't noticed the stamp of genius even on Stanley's forehead.

[*She takes off the blouse and stands in her pink silk brassiere and white skirt in the light through the portieres. The game has continued in undertones.*]

➔ Blanche is in the habit of taking refuge in bathing throughout the play. Why? Look out for further instances in the play.

in knots an uncomfortable feeling caused by a strong emotion such as anger, fear, excitement

awkward ['ɔːkwəd] embarrassed, lacking in social poise
courtesy ['kɜːtəsi] politeness and respect
custard dessert made of eggs and milk

wolf (AE, slang) a man who flirts aggressively with women, womanizer

precision bench *Präzisionswerkbank*
spare parts new parts for a machine or car made to replace old ones
plant factory

brassiere ['bræsiə], AE [brə'zɪr] (usu. bra) a piece of underwear worn by women to support their breasts
in undertones quietly and softly, not loudly

STELLA It isn't on his forehead and it isn't genius.

BLANCHE Oh. Well, what is it, and where? I would like to know.

STELLA It's a drive that he has. You're standing in the light, Blanche!

BLANCHE Oh, am I!

[She moves out of the yellow streak of light. Stella has removed her dress and put on a tight blue satin kimono.]

STELLA *[with girlish laughter]* You ought to see their wives.

BLANCHE *[laughingly]* I can imagine. Big, beefy things, I suppose.

STELLA You know that one upstairs? *[More laughter]* One time *[laughing]* the plaster – *[laughing]* cracked –

STANLEY You hens cut out that conversation in there!

STELLA You can't hear us.

STANLEY Well, you can hear me and I said to hush up!

STELLA This is my house and I'll talk as much as I want to!

BLANCHE Stella, don't start a row.

STELLA He's half drunk! – I'll be out in a minute.

[She goes into the bathroom. Blanche rises and crosses leisurely to a small white radio and turns it on.]

STANLEY Awright, Mitch, you in?

MITCH What? Oh! – No, I'm out!

[Blanche moves back into the streak of light. She raises her arms and stretches, as she moves indolently back to the chair. Rhumba music comes over the radio. Mitch rises at the table.]

STANLEY Who turned that on in there?

BLANCHE I did. Do you mind?

STANLEY Turn it off!

STEVE Aw, let the girls have their music.

PABLO Sure, that's good, leave it on!

STEVE Sounds like Xavier Cugat!

[Stanley jumps up and, crossing to the radio, turns it off. He stops short at the sight of Blanche in the chair. She returns his look without flinching. Then he sits again at the poker table. Two of the men have started arguing hotly.]

STEVE I didn't hear you name it.

PABLO Didn't I name it, Mitch?

MITCH I wasn't listenin'.

PABLO What were you doing, then?

STANLEY He was looking through them drapes. *[He jumps up and jerks roughly at curtains to close them.]* Now deal the hand over again and let's play cards or quit. Some people get ants when they win.

[Mitch rises as Stanley returns to his seat.]

---

streak thin stripe; a flash of light

beefy (informal) big, strong, and fat

plaster a substance used to cover walls with (*Putz*)

hen (slang) woman, a hen is a female chicken; an all-women party is called a "hen party"; an all-male party a "stag party"

row [raʊ] noisy quarrel, dispute

leisurely ['leʒəli], AE ['liːʒərli] without haste, in a relaxed manner

indolent ['ɪndələnt] (formal) lazy; (here) relaxed, easy

Xavier Cugat a Cuban bandleader, who popularised rhumba music and other Cuban dances in the United States in the 1940s

flinch to draw back (as from a blow) or to wince (as from pain)

name (here, in poker) to set or fix the stake

get ants (slang) to get so excited that you are unable to sit or stand still

STANLEY [*yelling*] Sit down!

MITCH I'm going to the "head". Deal me out.

PABLO Sure he's got ants now. Seven five-dollar bills in his pants pocket folded as tight as spitballs.

STEVE Tomorrow you'll see him at the cashier's window getting them changed into quarters.

STANLEY And when he goes home he'll deposit them one by one in a piggy bank his mother give him for Christmas. [*Dealing.*] This game is Spit in the Ocean.

[*Mitch laughs uncomfortably and continues through the portieres. He stops just inside.*]

BLANCHE [*softly*] Hello! The Little Boys' Room is busy right now.

MITCH We've – been drinking beer.

BLANCHE I hate beer.

MITCH It's – a hot weather drink.

BLANCHE Oh, I don't think so; it always makes me warmer. Have you got any cigs? [*She has slipped on the dark red satin wrapper.*]

MITCH Sure.

BLANCHE What kind are they?

MITCH Luckies.

BLANCHE Oh, good. What a pretty case. Silver?

MITCH Yes. Yes; read the inscription.

BLANCHE Oh, is there an inscription? I can't make it out. [*He strikes a match and moves closer*] Oh! [*reading with feigned difficulty*] "And if God choose,
I shall but love thee better – after – death!"
Why, that's from my favorite sonnet by Mrs. Browning!

MITCH You know it?

BLANCHE Certainly I do!

MITCH There's a story connected with that inscription.

BLANCHE It sounds like a romance.

MITCH A pretty sad one.

BLANCHE Oh?

MITCH The girl's dead now.

BLANCHE [*in a tone of deep sympathy*] *Oh!*

MITCH She knew she was dying when she give me this. A very strange girl, very sweet – very!

BLANCHE She must have been fond of you. Sick people have such deep, sincere attachments.

MITCH That's right, they certainly do.

BLANCHE Sorrow makes for sincerity, I think.

MITCH It sure brings it out in people.

BLANCHE The little there is belongs to people who have experienced some sorrow.

head (slang) toilet, WC
deal sb out (card games) not to give cards to a player
pants (AE) trousers (in BE pants means a piece of underwear, called underpants in AE)
spitball a piece of paper screwed up into a wad for throwing
cashier [kæ'ʃɪə] sb whose job it is to pay out or receive money (in a shop or a bank)
piggy bank a small container, often in the shape of a pig, with a slot for receiving coins
Spit in the Ocean kind of poker game
The Little Boys' Room (informal, humorous) men's toilet

➊ Blanche encounters Mitch. What do we learn about the two characters and their possible interaction from the first conversation they have? In this context, what is the function of poetry here? Relate it to Blanche's previous (and later) statements about herself.

wrapper a woman's dressing-gown
Luckies Lucky Strike cigarettes
inscription a piece of writing inscribed (written) on the surface of a stone, a coin, etc.
Mrs. Browning the English poet Elizabeth Barrett-Browning (1806–1861); the lines quoted are from her sonnet "How do I love thee? ...", No. 43 in her collection *Sonnets from the Portuguese* (1850)

attachment affection, devotion, feeling that you love sb dearly

positive certain, having no doubt
shuperficial (in imitation of her speech, which is a little thick) correctly: superficial
let out (AE) (a show, school, etc.) to end so that people can leave
orchard ['ɔ:tʃəd] an area of land where fruit trees are grown
extraction origin, descent
Huguenots ['hju:gəna:tz] French Protestants, mainly in the 16th and 17th centuries
adorable [ə'dɔ:rəbl] (colloquial) delightful, charming
Bourbon ['bʊəbən], also ['bɜ:bən] Bourbon Street in the French Quarter of New Orleans
adaptable able to adjust oneself to new circumstances
run down tired, worn out
gallantry polite manner (like a gallant: a nobleman at court)
grade school (AE) elementary school

MITCH I believe you are right about that.

BLANCHE I'm positive that I am. Show me a person who hasn't known any sorrow and I'll show you a shuperficial – Listen to me! My tongue is a little – thick! You boys are responsible for it. The show let out at eleven and we couldn't come home on account of the poker game so we had to go somewhere and drink. I'm not accustomed to having more than one drink. Two is the limit – and *three*! [*She laughs*] Tonight I had three.

STANLEY Mitch!

MITCH Deal me out I'm talking to Miss –

BLANCHE DuBois.

MITCH Miss DuBois?

BLANCHE It's a French name. It means woods and Blanche means white, so the two together mean white woods. Like an orchard in spring! You can remember it by that.

MITCH You're French?

BLANCHE We are French by extraction. Our first American ancestors were French Huguenots.

MITCH You are Stella's sister, are you not?

BLANCHE Yes, Stella is my precious little sister. I call her little in spite of the fact she's somewhat older than I. Just slightly. Less than a year. Will you do something for me?

MITCH Sure. What?

BLANCHE I bought this adorable little colored paper lantern at a Chinese shop on Bourbon. Put it over the light bulb! Will you, please?

MITCH Be glad to.

BLANCHE I can't stand a naked light bulb, any more than I can a rude remark or a vulgar action.

MITCH [*adjusting the lantern*] I guess we strike you as being a pretty rough bunch.

BLANCHE I'm very adaptable – to circumstances.

MITCH Well, that's a good thing to be. You are visiting Stanley and Stella?

BLANCHE Stella hasn't been so well lately, and I came down to help her for a while. She's very run down.

MITCH You're not –?

BLANCHE Married? No, no. I'm an old maid schoolteacher!

MITCH You may teach school but you're certainly not an old maid.

BLANCHE Thank you, sir! I appreciate your gallantry!

MITCH So you are in the teaching profession?

BLANCHE Yes. Ah, yes ...

MITCH Grade school or high school or –

STANLEY [*bellowing*] Mitch!

MITCH *Coming!*

BLANCHE Gracious, what lung-power! ... I teach high school. In Laurel.

MITCH What do you teach? What subject?

BLANCHE Guess!

MITCH I bet you teach art or music? [*Blanche laughs delicately*] Of course I could be wrong. You might teach arithmetic.

BLANCHE Never arithmetic, sir; never arithmetic! [*with a laugh*] I don't even know my multiplication tables! No, I have the misfortune of being an English instructor. I attempt to instill a bunch of bobby-soxers and drug-store Romeos with reverence for Hawthorne and Whitman and Poe!

MITCH I guess that some of them are more interested in other things.

BLANCHE How very right you are! Their literary heritage is not what most of them treasure above all else! But they're sweet things! And in the spring, it's touching to notice them making their first discovery of love! As if nobody had ever known it before!

[*The bathroom door opens and Stella comes out. Blanche continues talking to Mitch.*]

Oh! Have you finished? Wait – I'll turn on the radio.

[*She turns the knobs on the radio and it begins to play "Wien, Wien, nur du allein." Blanche waltzes to the music with romantic gestures. Mitch is delighted and moves in awkward imitation like a dancing bear.*

Stanley stalks fiercely through the portieres into the bedroom. He crosses to the small white radio and snatches it off the table. With a shouted oath, he tosses the instrument out the window.]

STELLA *Drunk – drunk – animal thing, you!* [*She rushes through to the poker table*] All of you – please go home! If any of you have one spark of decency in you –

BLANCHE [*wildly*] Stella, watch out, he's –

[*Stanley charges after Stella.*]

MEN: [*feebly*] Take it easy, Stanley. Easy, fellow. – Let's all –

STELLA You lay your hands on me and I'll –

[*She backs out of sight. He advances and disappears. There is the sound of a blow. Stella cries out. Blanche screams and runs into the kitchen. The men rush forward and there is grappling and cursing. Something is overturned with a crash.*]

BLANCHE [*shrilly*] My sister is going to have a baby!

MITCH This is terrible.

multiplication tables *Einmaleins*
instill (BE: instil) to put an idea, a principle, a feeling into sb's mind little by little
bobby-soxer (informal) a girl in her teens (in the 1940s)
Romeo a boy or man who is an ardent lover or a womaniser (from William Shakespeare's play *Romeo and Juliet)*
Hawthorne ['hɔ:θɔ:n] Nathaniel Hawthorne (1804–1854), an American novelist and short-story writer
Whitman Walt Whitman (1819–1892), an American poet
heritage traditional beliefs, customs, values of a country or family

knob [nɒb] a switch used to turn a radio on or off

How do you react to Stanley's violence? How does violence escalate in this scene? Why?

oath a curse, a swearword
toss to throw
spark a tiny rest
decency ['di:sənsi] the knowledge of what is proper and fitting in society

grapple to wrestle, to struggle in hand-to-hand fight

pinion to hold sb's arms or legs so that they cannot move freely
subside to become less active and stop
limp not firm or strong, no longer having any energy

blow one's top (slang) to fly into a rage, to lose one's temper

sons of bitches (esp. AE, impolite slang) an offensive expression for a man you are angry with (son of a bitch)
full tilt at full speed

"Paper Doll" song (1943) made popular by the Mills Brothers
blue sad and gloomy
polka dot a pattern of dots or spots
drawers [drɔːz] short undergarment, underpants
shudder to tremble violently (as in horror or disgust)

BLANCHE Lunacy, absolute lunacy!

MITCH Get him in here, men.

[*Stanley is forced, pinioned by the two men, into the bedroom. He nearly throws them off. Then all at once he subsides and is limp in their grasp.*

They speak quietly and lovingly to him and he leans his face on one of their shoulders.]

STELLA [*in a high, unnatural voice, out of sight*] I want to go away, I want to go away!

MITCH Poker shouldn't be played in a house with women.

[*Blanche rushes into the bedroom.*]

BLANCHE I want my sister's clothes! We'll go to that woman's upstairs!

MITCH Where is the clothes?

BLANCHE [*opening the closet*] I've got them! [*She rushes through to Stella*] Stella, Stella, precious! Dear, dear little sister, don't be afraid!

[*With her arms around Stella, Blanche guides her to the outside door and upstairs.*]

STANLEY [*dully*] What's the matter; what's happened?

MITCH You just blew your top, Stan.

PABLO He's okay, now.

STEVE Sure, my boy's okay!

MITCH Put him on the bed and get a wet towel.

PABLO I think coffee would do him a world of good, now.

STANLEY [*thickly*] I want water.

MITCH Put him under the shower!

[*The men talk quietly as they lead him to the bathroom.*]

STANLEY Let the rut go of me, you sons of bitches!

[*Sounds of blows are heard. The water goes on full tilt.*]

STEVE Let's get quick out of here!

[*They rush to the poker table and sweep up their winnings on their way out.*]

MITCH [*sadly but firmly*] Poker should not be played in a house with women.

[*The door closes on them and the place is still. The Negro entertainers in the bar around the corner play "Paper Doll" slow and blue. After a moment Stanley comes out of the bathroom dripping water and still in his clinging wet polka dot drawers.*]

STANLEY Stella! [*There is a pause*] My baby doll's left me!

[*He breaks into sobs. Then he goes to the phone and dials, still shuddering with sobs.*]

Eunice? I want my baby. [*He waits a moment; then he hangs up and dials again*] Eunice! I'll keep on ringin' until I talk with my baby!

[An indistinguishable shrill voice is heard. He hurls phone to floor. Dissonant brass and piano sounds as the rooms dim out to darkness and the outer walls appear in the night light. The "blue piano" plays for a brief interval.

Finally, Stanley stumbles half-dressed out to the porch and down the wooden steps to the pavement before the building. There he throws back his head like a baying hound and bellows his wife's name: "Stella! Stella, sweetheart! Stella!"]

STANLEY Stell-*lahhhhh!*

EUNICE [*calling down from the door of her upper apartment*] Quit that howling out there an' go back to bed!

STANLEY I want my baby down here. Stella, Stella!

EUNICE She ain't comin' down so you quit! Or you'll git th' law on you!

STANLEY Stella!

EUNICE You can't beat on a woman an' then call 'er back! She won't come! And her goin' t' have a baby! ... You stinker! You whelp of a Polack, you! I hope they do haul you in and turn the fire hose on you, same as the last time!

STANLEY [*humbly*] Eunice, I want my girl to come down with me!

EUNICE Hah! [*She slams her door.*]

STANLEY [*with heaven-splitting violence*] STELL-LAHHHHH!

[The low-tone clarinet moans. The door upstairs opens again. Stella slips down the rickety stairs in her robe. Her eyes are glistening with tears and her hair loose about her throat and shoulders. They stare at each other. Then they come together with low, animal moans. He falls to his knees on the steps and presses his face to her belly, curving a little with maternity. Her eyes go blind with tenderness as she catches his head and raises him level with her. He snatches the screen door open and lifts her off her feet and bears her into the dark flat.]

[Blanche comes out on the upper landing in her robe and slips fearfully down the steps.]

BLANCHE Where is my little sister? Stella? Stella?

[She stops before the dark entrance of her sister's flat. Then catches her breath as if struck. She rushes down to the walk before the house. She looks right and left as if for a sanctuary. The music fades away. Mitch appears from around the corner.]

MITCH Miss DuBois?

BLANCHE Oh!

MITCH All quiet on the Potomac now?

BLANCHE She ran downstairs and went back in there with him.

MITCH Sure she did.

indistinguishable [ɪndɪ'stɪŋgwɪʃbl] so similar that no difference can be made out
dissonant not in harmony

stumble to walk in an unsteady way

bay to bark

stinker (slang) a disgusting person

whelp a child (showing contempt, insulting; a whelp is a young dog, a puppy)
haul in (informal) to put into prison
fire hose *Feuerwehrschlauch*

moan to make a low and mournful sound of sorrow or pain
glisten to shine and look wet

level with even, of the same height

sanctuary ['sæŋktʃuəri] a place of refuge or protection (literally, a holy place designed for prayer and worship)
All quiet on the Potomac? [pə'təʊmæk] Is everything okay and in good order? (General George McClellan, 1826–1885, is supposed to have made this statement during the Civil War; the Potomac is a river)

BLANCHE I'm terrified!

MITCH Ho-ho! There's nothing to be scared of. They're crazy about each other.

BLANCHE I'm not used to such –

MITCH Naw, it's a shame this had to happen when you just got here. But don't take it serious.

BLANCHE Violence! Is so –

MITCH Set down on the steps and have a cigarette with me.

BLANCHE I'm not properly dressed.

MITCH That don't make no difference in the Quarter.

BLANCHE Such a pretty silver case.

MITCH I showed you the inscription, didn't I?

BLANCHE Yes. [*During the pause, she looks up at the sky*] There's so much – so much confusion in the world ... [*He coughs diffidently*] Thank you for being so kind! I need kindness now.

Different types of music punctuate the action throughout the play to such an extent that we may speak of a symbolic subtext. Go back to the preceding scenes and take note of those parts where music is used to accompany, and comment on, the action. Continue this for the rest of the play.

diffident timid, shy, not very confident

Mitch and Blanche, from Elia Kazan's film

Scene Four

It is early the following morning. There is a confusion of street cries like a choral chant.

Stella is lying down in the bedroom. Her face is serene in the early morning sunlight. One hand rests on her belly, rounding slightly with new maternity. From the other dangles a book of colored comics. Her eyes and lips have that almost narcotized tranquility that is in the faces of Eastern idols.

The table is sloppy with remains of breakfast and the debris of the preceding night, and Stanley's gaudy pyjamas lie across the threshold of the bathroom. The outside door is slightly ajar on a sky of summer brilliance.

Blanche appears at this door. She has spent a sleepless night and her appearance entirely contrasts with Stella's. She presses her knuckles nervously to her lips as she looks through the door, before entering.

chant a song, melody (in a simple liturgical manner)
serene [sə'riːn] clear, bright, untroubled, peaceful
dangle to hang loosely swinging back and forth
tranquility peacefulness, being free from agitation
Eastern idol ['aɪdl] a heathen deity from the East (the Orient)
sloppy very untidy, messy
debris ['debriː] bits and pieces of rubbish
gaudy bright and showy, but lacking in good taste
ajar slightly open
knuckle the joint of a finger (*Knöchel*)

➍ What does the following dialogue between Stella and Blanche add to our understanding of the two sisters?

BLANCHE Stella?

STELLA [*stirring lazily*] Hmmh?

[*Blanche utters a moaning cry and runs into the bedroom, throwing herself down beside Stella in a rush of hysterical tenderness.*]

BLANCHE Baby, my baby sister!

STELLA [*drawing away from her*] Blanche, what is the matter with you?

[*Blanche straightens up slowly and stands beside the bed looking down at her sister with knuckles pressed to her lips.*]

BLANCHE He's left?

STELLA Stan? Yes.

BLANCHE Will he be back?

STELLA He's gone to get the car greased. Why?

BLANCHE Why! I've been half crazy, Stella! When I found out you'd been insane enough to come back in here after what happened – I started to rush in after you!

grease to smear with an oily substance
insane crazy, mad

STELLA I'm glad you didn't.

BLANCHE What were you thinking of? [*Stella makes an indefinite gesture*] Answer me! What? What?

STELLA Please, Blanche! Sit down and stop yelling.

BLANCHE All right, Stella. I will repeat the question quietly now. How could you come back in this place last night? Why, you must have slept with him!

[*Stella gets up in a calm and leisurely way.*]

STELLA Blanche, I'd forgotten how excitable you are. You're making much too much fuss about this.

BLANCHE Am I?

fuss nervous, excited and unnecessary activity or agitation

powder-keg potential source of violence (a powder-keg is a barrel to store gunpowder)

slipper light shoe used for indoor wear (Careful! German "*Slipper*" is "slip-on shoe")

stove (chiefly AE) a piece of kitchen equipment on which you cook food (BE: cooker)

matter of fact unemotional

pavement (AE) the hard surface of a road (in BE "pavement" is the path at the side of a road for people to walk on, which is a "sidewalk" in AE)

tube *Röhre (Radio)*

fix (informal) a difficult situation

emphatic expressing one's opinions strongly and forcibly

incredulous [in'kredjʊləs] surprised and unwilling to believe

mess the state of being untidy or dirty

STELLA Yes, you are, Blanche. I know how it must have seemed to you and I'm awful sorry it had to happen, but it wasn't anything as serious as you seem to take it. In the first place, when men are drinking and playing poker anything can happen. It's always a powder-keg. He didn't know what he was doing ... He was as good as a lamb when I came back and he's really very, very ashamed of himself.

BLANCHE And that – that makes it all right?

STELLA No, it isn't all right for anybody to make such a terrible row, but – people do sometimes. Stanley's always smashed things. Why, on our wedding night – soon as we came in here – he snatched off one of my slippers and rushed about the place smashing the light bulbs with it.

BLANCHE He did – *what*?

STELLA He smashed all the light bulbs with the heel of my slipper! [*She laughs.*]

BLANCHE And you – you *let* him? Didn't *run*, didn't *scream*?

STELLA I was – sort of – thrilled by it. [*She waits for a moment.*] Eunice and you had breakfast?

BLANCHE Do you suppose I wanted my breakfast?

STELLA There's some coffee left on the stove.

BLANCHE You're so – matter of fact about it, Stella.

STELLA What other can I be? He's taken the radio to get it fixed. It didn't land on the pavement so only one tube was smashed.

BLANCHE And you are standing there smiling!

STELLA What do you want me to do?

BLANCHE Pull yourself together and face the facts.

STELLA What are they, in your opinion?

BLANCHE In my opinion? You're married to a madman!

STELLA No!

BLANCHE Yes, you are, your fix is worse than mine is! Only you're not being sensible about it. I'm going to *do* something. Get hold of myself and make myself a new life!

STELLA Yes?

BLANCHE But you've given in. And that isn't right, you're not old! You can get out.

STELLA [*slowly and emphatically*] I'm not in anything I want to get out of.

BLANCHE [*incredulously*] What – Stella?

STELLA I said I am not in anything that I have a desire to get out of. Look at the mess in this room! And those empty bottles! They went through two cases last night! He promised this morning that he was going to quit having these poker parties, but you know how long such a promise is going to keep.

Oh, well, it's his pleasure, like mine is movies and bridge. People have got to tolerate each other's habits, I guess.

BLANCHE I don't understand you. [*Stella turns toward her*] I don't understand your indifference. Is this a Chinese philosophy you've – cultivated?

STELLA Is what – what?

BLANCHE This – shuffling about and mumbling – 'One tube smashed – beer-bottles – mess in the kitchen!' – as if nothing out of the ordinary has happened! [*Stella laughs uncertainly and picking up the broom, twirls it in her hands.*]

BLANCHE Are you deliberately shaking that thing in my face?

STELLA No.

BLANCHE Stop it. Let go of that broom. I won't have you cleaning up for him!

STELLA Then who's going to do it? Are you?

BLANCHE I? I!

STELLA No, I didn't think so.

BLANCHE Oh, let me think, if only my mind would function! We've got to get hold of some money, that's the way out!

STELLA I guess that money is always nice to get hold of.

BLANCHE Listen to me. I have an idea of some kind. [*Shakily she twists a cigarette into her holder*] Do you remember Shep Huntleigh? [*Stella shakes her head.*] Of course you remember Shep Huntleigh. I went out with him at college and wore his pin for a while. Well –

STELLA Well?

BLANCHE I ran into him last winter. You know I went to Miami during the Christmas holidays?

STELLA No.

BLANCHE Well, I did. I took the trip as an investment, thinking I'd meet someone with a million dollars.

STELLA Did you?

BLANCHE Yes. I ran into Shep Huntleigh – I ran into him on Biscayne Boulevard, on Christmas Eve, about dusk ... getting into his car – Cadillac convertible; must have been a block long!

STELLA I should think it would have been – inconvenient in traffic!

BLANCHE You've heard of oil-wells?

STELLA Yes – remotely.

BLANCHE He has them, all over Texas. Texas is literally spouting gold in his pockets.

STELLA My, my.

BLANCHE Y'know how indifferent I am to money. I think of money in terms of what it does for you. But he could do it, he could certainly do it!

shuffle to move slowly and noisily, without lifting your feet
mumble to speak quietly and not very clearly so that people hardly understand you
twirl to spin, to turn rapidly in a circle

holder a cigarette-holder

pin an ornament that is fastened to sb's clothes (in the USA, given by a man to a girl to show his commitment to a relationship)

Biscayne Boulevard [ˌbɪ'skeɪn 'bʊləvɑːd] a main road in Miami, Florida
convertible a car with a top, usually of canvas, that you can fold back or remove

spout (of liquids like water or oil) to shoot out with force in a jet

races horse races

Western Union (AE) the name of a telegraph company
operator (here) a person who works on a telephone switchboard and who connects you

grab to pick up or snatch suddenly or hastily
Kleenex (brand name, AE) soft tissues

measly ['mi:zli] slight, small, skimpy
coin of the realm the currency used in a country (pound, dollar, euro, etc.)
allowance a fixed amount of money; pocket money
smooth things over to make problems and difficulties appear less serious
take to the streets to become a prostitute
low on funds to be short of money, cash
bromo (informal) a bromide, a pill to make sb feel calm again

STELLA Do what, Blanche?

BLANCHE Why – set us up in a – shop!

STELLA What kind of a shop?

BLANCHE Oh, a – shop of some kind! He could do it with half what his wife throws away at the races.

STELLA He's married?

BLANCHE Honey, would I be here if the man weren't married? [*Stella laughs a little. Blanche suddenly springs up and crosses to phone. She speaks shrilly*] How do I get Western Union? – Operator! Western Union!

STELLA That's a dial phone, honey.

BLANCHE I can't dial, I'm too –

STELLA Just dial O.

BLANCHE O?

STELLA Yes, "O" for Operator! [*Blanche considers a moment; then she puts the phone down.*]

BLANCHE Give me a pencil. Where is a slip of paper? I've got to write it down first – the message, I mean ...
[*She goes to the dressing table, and grabs up a sheet of Kleenex and an eyebrow pencil for writing equipment.*]
Let me see now ... [*She bites the pencil*] 'Darling Shep. Sister and I in desperate situation.'

STELLA I beg your pardon!

BLANCHE 'Sister and I in desperate situation. Will explain details later. Would you be interested in –?' [*She bites the pencil again*] 'Would you be – interested – in ...' [*She smashes the pencil on the table and springs up*] You never get anywhere with direct appeals!

STELLA [*with a laugh*] Don't be so ridiculous, darling!

BLANCHE But I'll think of something, I've *got* to think of – *something*! Don't, don't laugh at me, Stella! Please, please don't – I – I want you to look at the contents of my purse! Here's what's in it! [*She snatches her purse open*] Sixty-five measly cents in coin of the realm!

STELLA [*crossing to bureau*] Stanley doesn't give me a regular allowance, he likes to pay bills himself, but – this morning he gave me ten dollars to smooth things over. You take five of it, Blanche, and I'll keep the rest.

BLANCHE Oh, no. No, Stella.

STELLA [*insisting*] I know how it helps your morale just having a little pocket-money on you.

BLANCHE No, thank you – I'll take to the streets!

STELLA Talk sense! How did you happen to get so low on funds?

BLANCHE Money just goes – it goes places. [*She rubs her forehead*] Sometime today I've got to get hold of a bromo!

STELLA I'll fix you one now.

BLANCHE Not yet – I've got to keep thinking!

STELLA I wish you'd just let things go, at least for a – while ...

BLANCHE Stella, I can't live with him! You can, he's your husband. But how could I stay here with him, after last night, with, just those curtains between us?

STELLA Blanche, you saw him at his worst last night.

BLANCHE On the contrary, I saw him at his best! What such a man has to offer is animal force and he gave a wonderful exhibition of that! But the only way to live with such a man is to – go to bed with him! And that's your job – not mine!

STELLA After you've rested a little, you'll see it's going to work out. You don't have to worry about anything while you're here. I mean – expenses ...

BLANCHE I have to plan for us both, to get us both – out!

STELLA You take it for granted that I am in something that I want to get out of.

BLANCHE I take it for granted that you still have sufficient memory of Belle Reve to find this place and these poker players impossible to live with.

STELLA Well, you're taking entirely too much for granted.

BLANCHE I can't believe you're in earnest.

STELLA No?

BLANCHE I understand how it happened – a little. You saw him in uniform, an officer, not here but –

STELLA I'm not sure it would have made any difference where I saw him.

BLANCHE Now don't say it was one of those mysterious electric things between people! If you do I'll laugh in your face.

STELLA I am not going to say anything more at all about it!

BLANCHE All right, then, don't!

STELLA But there are things that happen between a man and a woman in the dark – that sort of make everything else seem – unimportant. [*Pause.*]

BLANCHE What you are talking about is brutal desire – just – Desire! – the name of that rattle-trap street-car that bangs through the Quarter, up one old narrow street and down another ...

STELLA Haven't you ever ridden on that street-car?

BLANCHE It brought me here. – Where I'm not wanted and where I'm ashamed to be ...

STELLA Then don't you think your superior attitude is a bit out of place?

BLANCHE I am not being or feeling at all superior, Stella. Believe me I'm not! It's just this. This is how I look at it. A

take for granted to believe that sth is certain and need not be discussed
sufficient [sə'fɪʃnt] enough

rattle-trap (AE) a vehicle that is old and in bad condition (*Klapperkiste*)
bang (here) to move making loud noise (*scheppern*)

man like that is someone to go out with – once – twice – three times when the devil is in you. But live with? Have a child by?

STELLA I have told you I love him.

BLANCHE Then I *tremble* for you! I just – tremble for you ...

STELLA I can't help your trembling if you insist on trembling! [*There is a pause.*]

BLANCHE May I – speak – plainly?

STELLA Yes, do. Go ahead. As plainly as you want to.

[*Outside, a train approaches. They are silent till the noise subsides. They are both in the bedroom.*
Under cover of the train's noise Stanley enters from outside. He stands unseen by the women, holding some packages in his arms, and overhears their following conversation. He wears an undershirt and grease-stained seersucker pants.]

Overhearing is a common device in drama. How is this passage to be arranged on the stage? What conclusions does the audience draw from this scene?

overhear to hear what people say accidentally (the people who speak do not know that you have heard them talking)
grease-stained with spots of oil or fat
seersucker ['sɪəˌsʌkə] a light cotton fabric (*kreppartiger Leinenstoff*)

BLANCHE Well – if you'll forgive me – he's *common!*

STELLA Why, yes, I suppose he is.

BLANCHE Suppose! You can't have forgotten that much of our bringing up, Stella, that you just *suppose* that any part of a gentleman's in his nature! *Not one particle, no!* Oh, if he was just – *ordinary*! Just *plain* – but good and wholesome, but – *no*. There's something downright – *bestial* – about him! You're hating me saying this, aren't you?

STELLA [*coldly*] Go on and say it all, Blanche.

Is Blanche's a fair summary of Stanley's character? Do you share her opinion? Remember that Stanley is listening in. What reactions can you expect? What does it mean that Stanley keeps hidden during Stella and Blanche's interchange?

BLANCHE He acts like an animal, has an animal's habits! Eats like one, moves like one, talks like one! There's even something – sub-human – something not quite to the stage of humanity yet! Yes, something – ape-like about him, like one of those pictures I've seen in – anthropological studies! Thousands and thousands of years have passed him right by, and there he is – Stanley Kowalski – survivor of the stone age! Bearing the raw meat home from the kill in the jungle! And you – *you* here – *waiting* for him! Maybe he'll strike you or maybe grunt and kiss you! That is, if kisses have been discovered yet! Night falls and the other apes gather! There in the front of the cave, all grunting like him, and swilling and gnawing and hulking! His poker night! – you call it – this party of apes! Somebody growls – some creature snatches at something – the fight is on! *God!* Maybe we are a long way from being made in God's image, but Stella – my sister – there has been *some* progress since then! Such things as art – as poetry and music – such kinds of new light have come into the world since then! In some kinds of people some tenderer feelings have had some little beginning! That we have got to make *grow!* And *cling* to,

wholesome ['həʊlsəm] healthy
bestial like a beast, primitive
anthropological [ˌænθrəʊpə'lodʒɪkl] concerning the scientific study of the human race
grunt to make a short, deep sound like a pig (in an effort or in annoyance)
swill drink alcohol greedily and in great quantities
gnaw [nɔː] (here) to eat like an animal
hulk (dialect) to lounge about in a heavy and clumsy manner (hulking: very big and clumsy)

and hold as our flag! In this dark march toward whatever it is we're approaching ... *Don't – don't hang back with the brutes!*

[*Another train passes outside. Stanley hesitates, licking his lips. Then suddenly he turns stealthily about and withdraws through front door. The women are still unaware of his presence. When the train has passed he calls through the closed front door.*]

STANLEY Hey! Hey, Stella!

STELLA [*who has listened gravely to Blanche*] Stanley!

BLANCHE Stell, I –

[*But Stella has gone to the front door. Stanley enters casually with his packages.*]

STANLEY Hiyuh, Stella. Blanche back?

STELLA Yes, she's back.

STANLEY Hiyuh, Blanche. [*He grins at her.*]

STELLA You must've got under the car.

STANLEY Them darn mechanics at Fritz's don't know their ass fr'm – Hey!

[*Stella has embraced him with both arms, fiercely, and full in the view of Blanche. He laughs and clasps her head to him. Over her head he grins through the curtains at Blanche.*]

[*As the lights fade away, with a lingering brightness on their embrace, the music of the "blue piano" and trumpet and drums is heard.*]

brute cruel, violent, insensitive person

stealthy ['stelθi] doing sth secretly or slyly

casual ['kæʒuəl] happening by chance, unplanned; relaxed and without a care in the world

darn (slang) damned

not to know one's ass fr'm (vulgar, slang) not to know anything (the English edition softens the expression and says: not to know one's can from third base; "third base" is a term taken from the language of baseball)

clasp to hold tightly, to grasp firmly

Scene Five

fan to make air move around (to make it cooler) by waving sth
peal of laughter loud, prolonged laughter

Blanche is seated in the bedroom fanning herself with a palm leaf as she reads over a just completed letter. Suddenly she bursts into a peal of laughter. Stella is dressing in the bedroom.

STELLA What are you laughing at, honey?

on the wing travelling
take a notion to have a mind to do, a desire or an inclination to do sth
swoop down on (here) to visit without warning
forewarned is forearmed it is better to know sth before it happens so that you can prepare yourself for it

BLANCHE Myself, myself, for being such a liar! I'm writing a letter to Shep. [*She picks up the letter*] "Darling Shep. I am spending the summer on the wing, making flying visits here and there. And who knows, perhaps I shall take a sudden notion to *swoop* down on *Dallas*! How would you feel about that? Ha-ha! [*She laughs nervously and brightly, touching her throat as if actually talking to Shep*] Forewarned is forearmed, as they say!" – How does that sound?

STELLA Uh-huh ...

the Gulf the Gulf of Mexico

BLANCHE [*going on nervously*] "Most of my sister's friends go north in the summer but some have homes on the Gulf and there has been a continued round of entertainments, teas, cocktails, and luncheons –"

[*A disturbance is heard upstairs at the Hubbells' apartment.*]

Why is the scene with Eunice and Steve introduced at this juncture?

STELLA Eunice seems to be having some trouble with Steve.

[*Eunice's voice shouts in terrible wrath.*]

wrath [rɔθ], AE [ræθ] anger
pull the wool over sb's eyes to trick or deceive sb by lying
the Four Deuces ['dju:sɪz] the name of a bar (in card games, deuce is a "two"; from the French word "deux")
vice squad the police department that deals with prostitution, drugs, etc.

EUNICE I heard about you and that blonde!

STEVE That's a damn lie!

EUNICE You ain't pulling the wool over my eyes! I wouldn't mind if you'd stay down at the Four Deuces, but you always going up.

STEVE Who ever seen me up?

EUNICE I seen you chasing her 'round the balcony – I'm gonna call the vice squad!

STEVE Don't you throw that at me!

aluminum AE for BE "aluminium"

EUNICE [*shrieking*] You hit me! I'm gonna call the police!

[*A clatter of aluminum striking a wall is heard, followed by a man's angry roar, shouts and overturned furniture. There is a crash; then a relative hush.*]

BLANCHE [*brightly*] Did he *kill* her?

daemonic [dɪ'mɒnɪk] like a demon, devilish, wild and cruel

[*Eunice appears on the steps in daemonic disorder.*]

STELLA No! She's coming downstairs.

EUNICE Call the police. I'm going to call the police! [*She rushes around the corner.*]

trot to move quickly, to hurry
register to realize, to notice

[*They laugh lightly. Stanley comes around the corner in his green and scarlet silk bowling shirt. He trots up the steps and bangs into the kitchen. Blanche registers his entrance with nervous gestures.*]

STANLEY What's a matter with Eun-uss?

STELLA She and Steve had a row. Has she got the police?

STANLEY Naw. She's gettin' a drink.

STELLA That's much more practical!

[*Steve comes down nursing a bruise on his forehead and looks in the door.*]

STEVE *She here?*

STANLEY Naw, naw. At the Four Deuces.

STEVE That rutting hunk! [*He looks around the corner a bit timidly, then turns with affected boldness and runs after her.*]

BLANCHE I must jot that down in my notebook. Ha-ha! I'm compiling a notebook of quaint little words and phrases I've picked up here.

STANLEY You won't pick up nothing here you ain't heard before.

BLANCHE Can I count on that?

STANLEY You can count on it up to five hundred.

BLANCHE That's a mighty high number. [*He jerks open the bureau drawer, slams it shut and throws shoes in a corner. At each noise Blanche winces slightly. Finally she speaks*] What sign were you born under?

STANLEY [*while he is dressing*] Sign?

BLANCHE Astrological sign. I bet you were born under Aries. Aries people are forceful and dynamic. They dote on noise! They love to bang things around! You must have had lots of banging around in the army and now that you're out, you make up for it by treating inanimate objects with such a fury!

[*Stella has been going in and out of closet during this scene. Now she pops her head out of the closet.*]

STELLA Stanley was born just five minutes after Christmas.

BLANCHE Capricorn – the Goat!

STANLEY What sign were *you* born under?

BLANCHE Oh, my birthday's next month, the fifteenth of September; that's under Virgo.

STANLEY What's Virgo?

BLANCHE Virgo is the Virgin.

STANLEY [*contemptuously*] Hah! [*He advances a little as he knots his tie*] Say, do you happen to know somebody named Shaw?

[*Her face expresses a faint shock. She reaches for the cologne bottle and dampens her handkerchief as she answers carefully.*]

BLANCHE Why, everybody knows somebody named Shaw!

STANLEY Well, this somebody named Shaw is under the impression he met you in Laurel, but I figure he must have got you mixed up with some other party because this other party is someone he met at a hotel called the Flamingo.

bruise [bruːz] a purple mark on your skin that you get after sb has hit you

hunk (informal) sb who is sexually attractive (usually, a man) because he is well-built and strong; (here, old-fashioned slang) an ugly, unpleasant woman

affected not natural, feigned

boldness fearlessness, willingness to take risks

jot down to make a brief, quick note

compile to gather and put together, to compose

bureau ['bjʊrəʊ] (AE) a piece of furniture with several drawers (for clothes etc.)

wince to draw back slightly, as in pain or alarm

Aries ['eəriːz] the first sign of the zodiac (astrological sign), March 22–April 19

dote to be excessively and foolishly fond of

inanimate [ɪn'ænimət] not living

Capricorn ['kæprɪkɔːn] the tenth sign of the zodiac, December 22–January 19

Goat the animal (*Ziege*), but also a reference to a lecherous = oversexed man (in Greek mythology, the goat is a symbol of excessive sexuality and fruitfulness)

Virgo ['vɜːgəʊ] the sixth sign of the zodiac, August 23–September 22; "virgo" is Latin for virgin

Why is Stanley contemptuous? (Go back to p. 29 and relate what happens there to the ongoing scene.)

contemptuous [kən'temptʃuəs] showing scorn and disrespect

cologne [kə'ləʊn] perfumed toilet water made of alcohol and aromatic oils (originally from the German city of Cologne)

figure (AE) to assume, to suppose

temple apart of sb's forehead (*Schläfe*)

penetrating sharp (sound or smell)

ounce (here, a unit of liquid measure) about 29 ml

luxurious [lʌk'ʒʊəriəs] (here) uncontrolled (normally "luxurious" refers to luxury, comfort, splendour and richness)

coo to make the soft, murmuring sound of doves or pigeons, to speak lovingly

rate (informal) to deserve

gossip idle talk and rumours about the private affairs of others

self-sufficient independent, having the necessary resources and qualities to get along without help

soft (of colours or light) not too bright and, therefore, pleasant

turn the trick (here) to be attractive to men

What are Blanche's fears? ➔ Why does Stella – a few lines down – say that Blanche is being morbid? Does Stella really understand her sister?

[*Blanche laughs breathlessly as she touches the cologne-dampened handkerchief to her temples.*]

BLANCHE I'm afraid he does have me mixed up with this "other party." The Hotel Flamingo is not the sort of establishment I would dare to be seen in!

STANLEY You know of it?

BLANCHE Yes, I've seen it and smelled it.

STANLEY You must've got pretty close if you could smell it.

BLANCHE The odor of cheap perfume is penetrating.

STANLEY That stuff you use is expensive?

BLANCHE Twenty-five dollars an ounce! I'm nearly out. That's just a hint if you want to remember my birthday! [*She speaks lightly but her voice has a note of fear.*]

STANLEY Shaw must've got you mixed up. He goes in and out of Laurel all the time so he can check on it and clear up any mistake.

[*He turns away and crosses to the portieres. Blanche closes her eyes as if faint. Her hand trembles as she lifts the handkerchief again to her forehead.*

[*Steve and Eunice come around corner. Steve's arm is around Eunice's shoulder and she is sobbing luxuriously and he is cooing love-words. There is a murmur of thunder as they go slowly upstairs in a tight embrace.*]

STANLEY [*to Stella*] I'll wait for you at the Four Deuces!

STELLA Hey! Don't I rate one kiss?

STANLEY Not in front of your sister.

[*He goes out. Blanche rises from her chair. She seems faint; looks about her with an expression of almost panic.*]

BLANCHE Stella! What have you heard about me?

STELLA Huh?

BLANCHE What have people been telling you about me?

STELLA Telling?

BLANCHE You haven't heard any – unkind – gossip about me?

STELLA Why, no, Blanche, of course not!

BLANCHE Honey, there was – a good deal of talk in Laurel.

STELLA About *you*, Blanche?

BLANCHE I wasn't so good the last two years or so, after Belle Reve had started to slip through my fingers.

STELLA All of us do things we –

BLANCHE I never was hard or sell-sufficient enough. When people are soft – soft people have got to shimmer and glow – they've got to put on soft colors, the colors of butterfly wings, and put a – paper lantern over the light ... It isn't enough to be soft. You've got to be soft *and attractive*. And I – I'm fading now! I don't know how much longer I can turn the trick.

[The afternoon has faded to dusk. Stella goes into the bedroom and turns on the light under the paper lantern. She holds a bottled soft drink in her hand.]

BLANCHE Have you been listening to me?

STELLA I don't listen to you when you are being morbid! [*She advances with the bottled coke.*]

BLANCHE [*with abrupt change to gaiety*] Is that coke for me?

STELLA Not for anyone else!

BLANCHE Why, you precious thing, you! Is it just coke?

STELLA [*turning*] You mean you want a shot in it!

BLANCHE Well, honey, a shot never does a coke any harm! Let me! You mustn't wait on me!

STELLA I like to wait on you, Blanche. It makes it seem more like home. [*She goes into the kitchen, finds a glass and pours a shot of whiskey into it.*]

BLANCHE I have to admit I love to be waited on ...

[She rushes into the bedroom. Stella goes to her with the glass. Blanche suddenly clutches Stella's free hand with a moaning sound and presses the hand to her lips. Stella is embarrassed by her show of emotion. Blanche speaks in a choked voice.]

You're – you're – so *good* to me! And I –

STELLA Blanche.

BLANCHE I know, I won't! You hate me to talk sentimental! But honey, *believe* I feel things more than I *tell* you! I *won't* stay long! I won't, I *promise* I –

STELLA Blanche!

BLANCHE [*hysterically*] I won't, I promise, *I'll* go! Go *soon*! I will *really*! I *won't* hang around until he – throws me out ...

STELLA Now will you stop talking foolish?

BLANCHE Yes, honey. Watch how you pour – that fizzy stuff foams over!

[Blanche laughs shrilly and grabs the glass, but her hand shakes so it almost slips from her grasp. Stella pours the coke into the glass. It foams over and spills. Blanche gives a piercing cry.]

STELLA [*shocked by the cry*] Heavens!

BLANCHE Right on my pretty white skirt!

STELLA Oh ... Use my hanky. Blot gently.

BLANCHE [*slowly recovering*] I know – gently – gently ...

STELLA Did it stain?

BLANCHE Not a bit. Ha-ha! Isn't that lucky? [*She sits down shakily, taking a grateful drink. She holds the glass in both hands and continues to laugh a little.*]

STELLA Why did you scream like that?

BLANCHE I don't know why I screamed! [*continuing nervously*] Mitch – Mitch is coming at seven. I guess I am just feeling

fade to lose one's colour, become less beautiful

morbid having a tendency to be interested in unpleasant and gloomy matters

gaiety ['geɪəti] cheerfulness, love of fun

choked (voice) hardly able to speak because one is so emotional (to choke is to be unable to breathe properly because sth is in your throat and blocks the passage of air)

fizzy (liquids) containing bubbles of gas, sparkling

foam over (fizzy liquids, beer etc.) *überschäumen*

piercing very loud and high-pitched

hanky short for "handkerchief"

blot to remove liquid by pressing cloth or paper on it

stain to leave a mark

nervous about our relations. [*She begins to talk rapidly and breathlessly*] He hasn't gotten a thing but a goodnight kiss, that's all I have given him, Stella. I want his respect. And men don't want anything they get too easy. But on the other hand men lose interest quickly. Especially when the girl is over – thirty. They think a girl over thirty ought to – the vulgar term is – "put out."... And I – I'm not "putting out." Of course he – he doesn't know – I mean I haven't informed him – of my real age!

put out (slang) (woman) to be promiscuous, engage in sexual intercourse with many men

STELLA Why are you sensitive about your age?

BLANCHE Because of hard knocks my vanity's been given. What I mean is – he thinks I'm sort of – prim and proper, you know! [*She laughs out sharply*] I want to *deceive* him enough to make him – want me ...

prim and proper stiffly formal, careful in the way one speaks and behaves

STELLA Blanche, do you want *him*?

BLANCHE I want to *rest*! I want to breathe quietly again! Yes – I *want* Mitch ... *very badly*! Just think! If it happens! I can leave here and not be anyone's problem ...

[*Stanley comes around the corner with a drink under his belt.*]

STANLEY [*bawling*] Hey, Steve! Hey, Eunice! Hey, Stella!

bawl to yell, to shout

[*There are joyous calls from above. Trumpet and drums are heard from around the corner.*]

STELLA [*kissing Blanche impulsively*] It *will* happen!

BLANCHE [*doubtfully*] It will?

STELLA It *will*! [*She goes across into the kitchen, looking back at Blanche.*] It will, honey, it *will* ... But don't take another drink!

[*Her voice catches as she goes out the door to meet her husband. Blanche sinks faintly back in her chair with her drink. Eunice shrieks with laughter and runs down the steps. Steve bounds after her with goat-like screeches and chases her around corner. Stanley and Stella twine arms as they follow, laughing.*

Dusk settles deeper. The music from the Four Deuces is slow and blue.]

catch (here) (voice) to pause because one is upset

twine arms *die Arme verschlingen*

BLANCHE Ah, me, ah, me, ah, me ...

[*Her eyes fall shut and the palm leaf fan drops from her fingers. She slaps her hand on the chair arm a couple of times. There is a little glimmer of lightning about the building.*

A Young Man comes along the street and rings the bell.]

What do we learn about Blanche in the ensuing scene with the young man? Does this contradict or support your previous view of Blanche? Could this passage be interpreted as a hint at the events to come (foreshadowing)?

BLANCHE Come in.

[*The Young Man appears through the portieres. She regards him with interest.*]

BLANCHE Well, well! What can I do for *you*?

YOUNG MAN I'm collecting for *The Evening Star*.

BLANCHE I didn't know that stars took up collections.

YOUNG MAN It's the paper.

BLANCHE I know. I was joking – feebly! Will you – have a drink?

YOUNG MAN No, ma'am. No, thank you. I can't drink on the job.

BLANCHE Oh, well, now, let's see ... No, I don't have a dime! I'm not the lady of the house. I'm her sister from Mississippi. I'm one of those poor relations you've heard about.

YOUNG MAN That's all right. I'll drop by later. [*He starts to go out. She approaches a little.*]

BLANCHE Hey! [*He turns back shyly. She puts a cigarette in a long holder*] Could you give me a light? [*She crosses toward him. They meet at the door between the two rooms.*]

YOUNG MAN Sure. [*He takes out a lighter*] This doesn't always work.

BLANCHE It's temperamental? [*It flares*] Ah! – thank you. [*He starts away again*] Hey! [*He turns again, still more uncertainly. She goes close to him*] Uh – what time is it?

YOUNG MAN Fifteen of seven, ma'am.

BLANCHE So late? Don't you just love these long rainy afternoons in New Orleans when an hour isn't just an hour – but a little piece of eternity dropped into your hands – and who knows what to do with it? [*She touches his shoulders.*] You – uh – didn't get wet in the rain?

YOUNG MAN No, ma'am. I stepped inside.

BLANCHE In a drug store? And had a soda?

YOUNG MAN Uh-huh.

BLANCHE Chocolate?

YOUNG MAN No, ma'am. Cherry.

BLANCHE [*laughing*] Cherry!

YOUNG MAN A cherry soda.

BLANCHE You make my mouth water. [*She touches his cheek lightly, and smiles. Then she goes to the trunk.*]

YOUNG MAN Well, I'd better be going –

BLANCHE [*stopping him*] Young man!

[*He turns. She takes a large, gossamer scarf from the trunk and drapes it about her shoulders.*]

[*In the ensuing pause, the "blue piano" is heard. It continues through the rest of this scene and the opening of the next. The young man clears his throat and looks yearningly at the door.*]

Young man! Young, young, young man! Has anyone ever told you that you look like a young Prince out of the Arabian Nights?

[*The Young Man laughs uncomfortably and stands like a bashful kid. Blanche speaks softly to him.*]

Well, you do, honey lamb! Come here. I want to kiss you, just once, softly and sweetly on your mouth!

dime (AE) a ten-cent coin

temperamental excitable, unpredictable

flare to burn for a short time

fifteen of seven (AE) quarter to seven

gossamer a very thin, soft, filmy cloth

ensue [ɪn'sjuː] to follow immediately

clear one's throat to cough so as to be able to speak with a clear voice

Arabian Nights *Märchen aus 1001 Nacht*

bashful shy, easily embarrassed

[*Without waiting for him to accept, she crosses quickly to him and presses her lips to his.*]
Now run along, now, quickly! It would be nice to keep you, but I've got to be good – and keep my hands off children.
[*He stares at her a moment. She opens the door for him and blows a kiss at him as he goes down the steps with a dazed look. She stands there a little dreamily after he has disappeared. Then Mitch appears around the corner with a bunch of roses.*]

BLANCHE [*gaily*] Look who's coming! My Rosenkavalier! Bow to me first ... now present them! *Ahhhh – Merciiii!*
[*She looks at him over them, coquettishly pressing them to her lips. He beams at her selfconsciously.*]

dazed confused, bewildered, unable to think clearly because of shock

My Rosenkavalier allusion to Richard Strauss's opera *Der Rosenkavalier* (1911)
coquettish [ko'ketɪʃ] flirting
beam to smile happily
selfconscious (usu. self-conscious) worried and embarrassed, wondering what others may think about you (Careful! The German "*selbstbewusst*" is confident, self-confident, self-assured.)

"My Rosenkavalier!"
From Elia Kazan's film

Scene Six

It is about two A.M. on the same evening. The outer wall of the building is visible. Blanche and Mitch come in. The utter exhaustion which only a neurasthenic personality can know is evident in Blanche's voice and manner. Mitch is stolid but depressed. They have probably been out to the amusement park on Lake Pontchartrain, for Mitch is bearing, upside down, a plaster statuette of Mae West, the sort of prize won at shooting-galleries and carnival games of chance.

BLANCHE [*stopping lifelessly at the steps*] Well –
[*Mitch laughs uneasily.*]
Well ...

MITCH I guess it must be pretty late – and you're tired.

BLANCHE Even the hot tamale man has deserted the street, and he hangs on till the end. [*Mitch laughs uneasily again*] How will you get home?

MITCH I'll walk over to Bourbon and catch an owl-car.

BLANCHE [*laughing grimly*] Is that streetcar named Desire still grinding along the tracks at this hour?

MITCH [*heavily*] I'm afraid you haven't gotten much fun out of this evening, Blanche.

BLANCHE I spoiled it for *you*.

MITCH No, you didn't, but I felt all the time that I wasn't giving you much – entertainment.

BLANCHE I simply couldn't rise to the occasion. That was all. I don't think I've ever tried so hard to be gay and made such a dismal mess of it. I get ten points for trying! – I *did* try.

MITCH Why did you try if you didn't feel like it, Blanche?

BLANCHE I was just obeying the law of nature.

MITCH Which law is that?

BLANCHE The one that says the lady must entertain the gentleman – or no dice! See if you can locate my door-key in this purse. When I'm so tired my fingers are all thumbs!

MITCH [*rooting in her purse*] This it?

BLANCHE No, honey, that's the key to my trunk which I must soon be packing.

MITCH You mean you are leaving here soon?

BLANCHE I've outstayed my welcome.

MITCH This it?
[*The music fades away.*]

BLANCHE Eureka! Honey, you open the door while I take a last look at the sky. [*She leans on the porch rail. He opens the door and stands awkwardly behind her.*] I'm looking for the Pleia-

neurasthenic [ˌnjʊərəs'θenɪk] irritable and anxious as a result of weakness and exhaustion of the nervous system
stolid impassive, unemotional, unexcitable
statuette [ˌstætʃu'et] a small statue
Lake Pontchartrain ['pɒntʃətreɪn] a lake north of New Orleans
Mae West [meɪ] (1892–1980) American actress and sex symbol in the 1930s and 1940s

Watch out for indications that Blanche is leading Mitch on. Pay close attention to the stage directions. How would a director use body language and pitch of voice in this scene?

shooting gallery at an amusement park, a place for practising shooting at targets to win a prize
carnival (here) an amusement park
game of chance a game in which you risk money on the result (*Glückspiel*)
owl-car [aʊl] a late-night train or streetcar
grind [graɪnd] to move with an unpleasant noise
dismal [z] depressing, causing misery
no dice (colloquial) no luck
my fingers are all thumbs I am so awkward that I drop everything
root to search for, to rummage
outstay one's welcome to stay longer than one is welcome
Eureka [juə'riːkə] (exclamation) I've got it (to show how glad you are that you have found sth)
Pleiades ['plaɪədiːz] a cluster of stars in the constellation Taurus (six are readily visible, the seventh seems to have faded from sight; they represent the daughters of Atlas)

des, the Seven Sisters, but these girls are not out tonight. Oh, yes they are, there they are! God bless them! All in a bunch going home from their little bridge party ... Y'get the door open? Good boy! I guess you – want to go now ... [*He shuffles and coughs a little.*]

MITCH Can I – uh – kiss you – goodnight?

BLANCHE Why do you always ask me if you may?

MITCH I don't know whether you want me to or not.

BLANCHE Why should you be so doubtful?

MITCH That night when we parked by the lake and I kissed you, you –

BLANCHE Honey, it wasn't the kiss I objected to. I liked the kiss very much. It was the other little – familiarity – that I – felt obliged to – discourage ... I didn't resent it! Not a bit in the world! In fact, I was somewhat flattered that you – desired me! But, honey, you know as well as I do that a single girl, a girl alone in the world, has got to keep a firm hold on her emotions or she'll be lost!

MITCH [*solemnly*] Lost?

BLANCHE I guess you are used to girls that like to be lost. The kind that get lost immediately, on the first date!

MITCH I like you to be exactly the way that you are, because in all my – experience – I have never known anyone like you. [*Blanche looks at him gravely; then she bursts into laughter and then claps a hand to her mouth.*]

MITCH Are you laughing at me?

BLANCHE No, honey. The lord and lady of the house have not yet returned, so come in. We'll have a night-cap. Let's leave the lights off. Shall we?

MITCH You just – do what you want to.

[*Blanche precedes him into the kitchen. The outer wall of the building disappears and the interiors of the two rooms can be dimly seen.*]

BLANCHE [*remaining in the first room*] The other room's more comfortable – go on in. This crashing around in the dark is my search for some liquor.

MITCH You want a drink?

BLANCHE I want *you* to have a drink! You have been so anxious and solemn all evening, and so have I; we have both been anxious and solemn and now for these few last remaining moments of our lives together – I want to create – *joie de vivre*! I'm lighting a candle.

MITCH That's good.

BLANCHE We are going to be very Bohemian. We are going to pretend that we are sitting in a little artists' cafe on the Left Bank

---

object to to protest, to be opposed to, to mind

resent to feel angry and hurt about sth that you consider unfair

night-cap (informal) alcoholic drink taken before going to bed or to end a party

precede to go before

joie de vivre (French) joy of living

Bohemian [bəʊˈhiːmiən] (artists etc.) living in an unconventional and nonconforming way (originally, an inhabitant of the Czech province of Bohemia)

the Left Bank (in Paris, the left bank of the Seine) the artists' quarter in Paris

in Paris! [*She lights a candle stub and puts it in a bottle.*] *Je suis la Dame aux Camellias! Vous êtes – Armand!* Understand French?

MITCH [*heavily*] Naw. Naw. I –

BLANCHE *Voulez-vous couchez avec moi ce soir? Vous ne comprenez pas? Ah, quelle dommage!* – I mean it's a damned good thing ... I've found some liquor. Just enough for two shots without any dividends, honey ...

MITCH [*heavily*] That's – good.

[*She enters the bedroom with the drinks and the candle*]

BLANCHE Sit down! Why don't you take off your coat and loosen your collar?

MITCH I better leave it on.

BLANCHE No. I want you to be comfortable.

MITCH I am ashamed of the way I perspire. My shirt is sticking to me.

BLANCHE Perspiration is healthy. If people didn't perspire they would die in five minutes. [*She takes his coat from him*] This is a nice coat. What kind of material is it?

MITCH They call that stuff alpaca.

BLANCHE Oh. Alpaca.

MITCH It's very light weight alpaca.

BLANCHE Oh. Light weight alpaca.

MITCH I don't like to wear a wash-coat even in summer because I sweat through it.

BLANCHE Oh.

MITCH And it don't look neat on me. A man with a heavy build has got to be careful of what he puts on him so he don't look too clumsy.

BLANCHE You are not too heavy.

MITCH You don't think I am?

BLANCHE You are not the delicate type. You have a massive bone-structure and a very imposing physique.

MITCH Thank you. Last Christmas I was given a membership to the New Orleans Athletic Club.

BLANCHE Oh, good.

MITCH It was the finest present I ever was given. I work out there with the weights and I swim and keep myself fit. When I started there, I was getting soft in the belly but now my belly is hard. It is so hard now that a man can punch me in the belly and it don't hurt me. Punch me! Go on! See? [*She pokes lightly at him.*]

BLANCHE Gracious. [*Her hand touches her chest.*]

MITCH Guess how much I weigh, Blanche?

BLANCHE Oh, I'd say in the vicinity of – one hundred and eighty?

stub the short length of sth much longer that has been used up

Je suis la Dame aux Camellias! Vous êtes – Armand (correctly: Camélias) I am the Lady of the Camellias. You are Armand (an allusion to Alexandre Dumas' novel *La Dame aux Camélias* from 1848; Armand is the lover of the Lady in the novel)

voulez-vous couchez avec moi ce soir? Vous ne comprenez pas? Ah, quelle dommage! (correctly: coucher; quel) Would you like to sleep with me tonight? You don't understand? What a pity.

without any dividends (here) and not a drop more

perspire to sweat

alpaca [æl'pækə] type of wool made from a type of South American llama (called alpaca)

wash-coat (AE) a flannel (soft, lightweight cloth) coat

physique [fɪ'ziːk] strength, form or appearance of a body

work out (AE) to train, to exercise to improve one's athletic skill

in the vicinity of [və'sɪnəti] close to; about

one hundred and eighty 180 pounds (a pound is 453.59 g)

MITCH Guess again.

BLANCHE Not that much?

MITCH No. More.

BLANCHE Well, you're a tall man and you can carry a good deal of weight without looking awkward.

MITCH I weigh two hundred and seven pounds and I'm six feet one and onehalf inches tall in my bare feet – without shoes on. And that is what I weigh stripped.

BLANCHE Oh, my goodness, me! It's awe-inspiring.

MITCH [*embarrassed*] My weight is not a very interesting subject to talk about. [*He hesitates for a moment*] What's yours?

BLANCHE My weight?

MITCH Yes.

BLANCHE Guess!

MITCH Let me lift you.

BLANCHE Samson! Go on, lift me. [*He comes behind her and puts his hands on her waist and raises her lightly off the ground*] Well?

MITCH You are light as a feather.

BLANCHE Ha-ha! [*He lowers her but keeps his hands on her waist. Blanche speaks with an affectation of demureness*] You may release me now.

MITCH Huh?

BLANCHE [*gaily*] I said unhand me, sir. [*He fumblingly embraces her. Her voice sounds gently reproving*] Now, Mitch. Just because Stanley and Stella aren't at home is no reason why you shouldn't behave like a gentleman.

MITCH Just give me a slap whenever I step out of bounds.

BLANCHE That won't be necessary. You're a natural gentleman, one of the very few that are left in the world. I don't want you to think that I am severe and old maid school-teacherish or anything like that. It's just – well –

MITCH Huh?

BLANCHE I guess it is just that I have – old-fashioned ideals! [*She rolls her eyes, knowing he cannot see her face. Mitch goes to the front door. There is a considerable silence between them. Blanche sighs and Mitch coughs selfconsciously.*]

MITCH [*finally*] Where's Stanley and Stella tonight?

BLANCHE They have gone out. With Mr. and Mrs. Hubbell upstairs.

MITCH Where did they go?

BLANCHE I think they were planning to go to a midnight prevue at Loew's State.

MITCH We should all go out together some night.

BLANCHE No. That wouldn't be a good plan.

foot 30.48 cm
inch 2.54 cm
stripped naked, without clothes

Samson in the Bible, a man noted for his great strength

demureness [dɪ'mjʊənəs] a show of affected modesty or shyness, coyness

unhand (humorous) to set sb free
fumbling clumsy and unskilful
reprove to express disapproval or criticism

step out of bounds to do sth that is forbidden

prevue ['priːvjuː] (AE) a preview, restricted showing of a movie before it is shown to the general public
Loew's State [ləʊv] the name of a cinema in New Orleans

MITCH Why not?

BLANCHE You are an old friend of Stanley's?

MITCH We was together in the Two-forty-first.

BLANCHE I guess he talks to you frankly?

MITCH Sure.

BLANCHE Has he talked to you about me?

MITCH Oh – not very much.

BLANCHE The way you say that, I suspect that he has.

MITCH No, he hasn't said much.

BLANCHE But what he *has* said. What would you say his attitude toward me was?

MITCH Why do you want to ask that?

BLANCHE Well –

MITCH Don't you get along with him?

BLANCHE What do you think?

MITCH I don't think he understands you.

BLANCHE That is putting it mildly. If it weren't for Stella about to have a baby, I wouldn't be able to endure things here.

MITCH He isn't – nice to you?

BLANCHE He is insufferably rude. Goes out of his way to offend me.

MITCH In what way, Blanche?

BLANCHE Why, in every conceivable way.

MITCH I'm surprised to hear that.

BLANCHE Are you?

MITCH Well, I – don't see how anybody could be rude to you.

BLANCHE It's really a pretty frightful situation. You see, there's no privacy here. There's just these portieres between the two rooms at night. He stalks through the rooms in his underwear at night. And I have to ask him to close the bathroom door. That sort of commonness isn't necessary. You probably wonder why I don't move out. Well, I'll tell you frankly. A teacher's salary is barely sufficient for her living-expenses. I didn't save a penny last year and so I had to come here for the summer. That's why I have to put up with my sister's husband. And he has to put up with me, apparently so much against his wishes ... Surely he must have told you how much he hates me!

MITCH I don't think he hates you.

BLANCHE He hates me. Or why would he insult me? The first time I laid eyes on him I thought to myself, that man is my executioner! That man will destroy me, unless –

MITCH Blanche –

BLANCHE Yes, honey?

MITCH Can I ask you a question?

the Two-forty-first the name of an army regiment or division

endure [ɪn'djʊə] to put up with, to tolerate
enduring, endurable

insufferable [ɪn'sʌfərəbl] unbearable, intolerable

conceivable [kən'si:vəbl] that can be understood or believed, imaginable

put up with to bear, to suffer patiently, to tolerate

insult to treat sb with great disrespect; to make remarks that are meant to be hurtful
executioner [ˌeksɪ'kju:ʃnə] sb who carries out the death penalty

Mitch's mother never appears in person. What role does she play? Can she affect the budding relationship between Mitch and Blanche?

settled to be established in marriage or business; (here) to be married

devotion loyalty and deep affection
pass on (euphemism) to die

sill *Fensterbank*

delude [dɪˈluːd] to fool or deceive sb by holding out false promises

effeminate [ɪˈfemɪnət] (man) unmanly, not virile, womanish

BLANCHE Yes. What?

MITCH How old are you?

[*She makes a nervous gesture.*]

BLANCHE Why do you want to know?

MITCH I talked to my mother about you and she said, "How old is Blanche?" And I wasn't able to tell her. [*There is another pause.*]

BLANCHE You talked to your mother about me?

MITCH Yes.

BLANCHE Why?

MITCH I told my mother how nice you were, and I liked you.

BLANCHE Were you sincere about that?

MITCH You know I was.

BLANCHE Why did your mother want to know my age?

MITCH Mother is sick.

BLANCHE I'm sorry to hear it. Badly?

MITCH She won't live long. Maybe just a few months.

BLANCHE Oh.

MITCH She worries because I'm not settled.

BLANCHE Oh.

MITCH She wants me to be settled down before she – [*His voice is hoarse and he clears his throat twice, shuffling nervously around with his hands in and out of his pockets.*]

BLANCHE You love her very much, don't you?

MITCH Yes.

BLANCHE I think you have a great capacity for devotion. You will be lonely when she passes on, won't you? [*Mitch clears his throat and nods.*] I understand what that is.

MITCH To be lonely?

BLANCHE I loved someone, too, and the person I loved I lost.

MITCH Dead? [*She crosses to the window and sits on the sill, looking out. She pours herself another drink.*] A man?

BLANCHE He was a boy, just a boy, when I was a very young girl. When I was sixteen, I made the discovery – love. All at once and much, much too completely. It was like you suddenly turned a blinding light on something that had always been half in shadow, that's how it struck the world for me. But I was unlucky. Deluded. There was something different about the boy, a nervousness, a softness and tenderness which wasn't like a man's, although he wasn't the least bit effeminate looking – still – that thing was there ... He came to me for help. I didn't know that. I didn't find out anything till after our marriage when we'd run away and come back and all I knew was I'd failed him in some mysterious way and wasn't able to give the help he needed but couldn't speak of! He was in the quicksands and clutching at me – but I wasn't holding him out, I was slipping in with him! I didn't know that. I didn't know anything except I loved him unendurably but without being able to help him or help myself. Then I found out. In the worst of all possible ways. By coming suddenly into a room that I thought was empty – which wasn't empty, but had two people in it ... the boy I had married and an older man who had been his friend for years ...

[*A locomotive is heard approaching outside. She claps her hands to her ears and crouches over. The headlight of the locomotive glares into the room as it thunders past. As the noise recedes she straightens slowly and continues speaking.*]

Afterwards we pretended that nothing had been discovered. Yes, the three of us drove out to Moon Lake Casino, very drunk and laughing all the way.

[*Polka music sounds, in a minor key faint with distance.*]

We danced the Varsouviana! Suddenly in the middle of the dance the boy I had married broke away from me and ran out of the casino. A few moments later – a shot!

[*The polka stops abruptly.*]

[*Blanche rises stiffly. Then, the polka resumes in a major key.*]

I ran out – all did! – all ran and gathered about the terrible thing at the edge of the lake! I couldn't get near for the crowding. Then somebody caught my arm. "Don't go any closer! Come back! You don't want to see!" See? See what! Then I heard voices say – Allan! Allan! The Grey boy! He'd stuck the revolver into his mouth, and fired – so that the back of his head had been – blown away!

[*She sways and covers her face.*]

It was because – on the dance-floor – unable to stop myself – I'd suddenly said – "I saw! I know! You disgust me ..." And then the searchlight which had been turned on the world was turned off again and never for one moment since has there been any light that's stronger than this – kitchen – candle ...

[*Mitch gets up awkwardly and moves toward her a little. The polka music increases. Mitch stands beside her.*]

MITCH [*drawing her slowly into his arms*] You need somebody. And I need somebody too. Could it be – you and me, Blanche?

[*She stares at him vacantly for a moment. Then with a soft cry huddles in his embrace. She makes a sobbing effort to speak but the words won't come. He kisses her forehead and her eyes and finally her lips. The polka tune fades out. Her breath is drawn and released in long, grateful sobs.*]

BLANCHE Sometimes – there's God – so quickly!

quicksand loose, wet, deep sand in which an object may easily be engulfed (sink)
unendurable [ˌʌnɪn'djʊərəbl] too painful to bear

crouch to bend low with the limbs drawn close to the body
recede to become less; to become more distant

casino (here) a public building for dancing etc.; more often, the term refers to a building that offers games of chance and gambling
minor key *Molltonart* (cf. major key: *Durtonart*)
Varsouviana a Polish dance (like a mazurka)

sway to move slowly from one side to the other
disgust to cause sb to feel sick, to be sickening and repulsive, to be distasteful

How do you react to Blanche's story of her marriage? Why does she say to her husband, "You disgust me." What has she found out? In what way do her marriage and its aftermath still touch her? Read the stage directions carefully, especially those bits that refer to sound effects.

vacant ['veɪkənt] empty, expressionless
huddle to draw or press close to sb from cold or fear to be comforted, to nestle

Scene Seven

It is late afternoon in mid-September.

The portieres are open and a table is set for a birthday supper, with cake and flowers.

Stella is completing the decorations as Stanley comes in.

STANLEY What's all this stuff for?

STELLA Honey, it's Blanche's birthday.

STANLEY She here?

STELLA In the bathroom.

STANLEY [*mimicking*] "Washing out some things"?

STELLA I reckon so.

STANLEY How long she been in there?

STELLA All afternoon.

STANLEY [*mimicking*] "Soaking in a hot tub"?

STELLA Yes.

STANLEY Temperature 100 on the nose, and she soaks herself in a hot tub.

STELLA She says it cools her off for the evening.

STANLEY And you run out an' get her cokes, I suppose? And serve 'em to Her Majesty in the tub? [*Stella shrugs*] Set down here a minute.

STELLA Stanley, I've got things to do.

STANLEY Set down! I've got th' dope on your big sister, Stella.

STELLA Stanley, stop picking on Blanche.

STANLEY That girl calls *me* common!

STELLA Lately you been doing all you can think of to rub her the wrong way, Stanley, and Blanche is sensitive and you've got to realize that Blanche and I grew up under very different circumstances than you did.

STANLEY So I been told. And told and told and told! You know she's been feeding us a pack of lies here?

STELLA No, I don't, and –

STANLEY Well, she has, however. But now the cat's out of the bag! I found out some things!

STELLA What – things?

STANLEY Things I already suspected. But now I got proof from the most reliable sources – which I have checked on! [*Blanche is singing in the bathroom a saccharine popular ballad which is used contrapuntally with Stanley's speech.*]

STELLA [*to Stanley*] Lower your voice!

STANLEY Some canary-bird, huh!

STELLA Now please tell me quietly what you think you've found out about my sister.

---

mimic to imitate in speech and action (so as to ridicule sb)
reckon (AE) to suppose

temperature 100 100° Fahrenheit, that is, about 38° Celsius
on the nose (AE, informal) precisely

shrug to draw up one's shoulders to show indifference or doubt

dope (AE, slang) information

pick on (informal) to single out for criticism, to annoy

rub sb the wrong way to annoy, to irritate, to make sb angry

feed sb a pack of lies (informal) to tell sb a lot of lies

saccharine ['sækəriːn] (AE) too sweet, syrupy
contrapuntal [ˌkontraˈpʌntl] *kontrapunktisch*
canary-bird [kəˈneəri] (here) singer (canary: *Kanarienvogel*)

What effect is achieved by having Blanche sing contrapuntally with Stanley's revelations. What do the stage directions say?

STANLEY Lie Number One: All this squeamishness she puts on! You should just know the line she's been feeding to Mitch. He thought she had never been more than kissed by a fellow! But Sister Blanche is no lily! Ha-ha! Some lily she is!

STELLA What have you heard and who from?

STANLEY Our supply-man down at the plant has been going through Laurel for years and he knows all about her and everybody else in the town of Laurel knows all about her. She is as famous in Laurel as if she was the President of the United States, only she is not respected by any party! This supply-man stops at a hotel called the Flamingo.

BLANCHE [*singing blithely*]

"Say, it's only a paper moon,
Sailing over a cardboard sea –
But it wouldn't be make-believe
If you believed in me!"

STELLA What about the – Flamingo?

STANLEY She stayed there, too.

STELLA My sister lived at Belle Reve.

STANLEY This is after the home-place had slipped through her lily-white fingers! She moved to the Flamingo! A second-class hotel which has the advantage of not interfering in the private social life of the personalities there! The Flamingo is used to all kinds of goings-on. But even the management of the Flamingo was impressed by Dame Blanche! In fact they was so impressed by Dame Blanche that they requested her to turn in her room-key – for permanently! This happened a couple of weeks before she showed here.

BLANCHE [*singing*]

"It's a Barnum and Bailey world,
Just as phony as it can be –
But it wouldn't be make-believe
If you believed in me!"

STELLA What – contemptible – lies!

STANLEY Sure, I can see how you would be upset by this. She pulled the wool over your eyes as much as Mitch's!

STELLA It's pure invention! There's not a word of truth in it and if I were a man and this creature had dared to invent such things in my presence –

BLANCHE [*singing*]

"Without your love,
It's a honky-tonk parade!
Without your love,
It's a melody played,
In a penny arcade ..."

squeamishness state of being easily shocked or offended; oversensitiveness

feed sb a line (informal) to try to persuade sb with an insincere story

lily a plant with a white flower (a symbol of purity and innocence)

supply-man sb who buys materials and provisions for a factory or a company

blithe [blaɪð] carefree, cheerful

say, it's only a paper moon a famous jazz song from 1932

make-believe pretence, fanciful belief that sth is true and real

➊ Are you surprised by Stanley's discovery?

interfere to meddle, to involve oneself deliberately in a situation where one is not wanted

dame (ironical) a title given to a woman in authority or who has been knighted

Barnum and Bailey a famous American circus company

phony (informal) not genuine, false, fake

contemptible worthless, not deserving any respect

pull the wool over sb's eyes (informal) to deceive or trick sb

honky-tonk (AE, slang) a cheap and noisy nightclub; a bar where country music is played

penny arcade [ɑːˈkeɪd] a hall in an amusement park, with coin-operated game machines, peep shows, photography booths, etc.

put on an act to pretend to have particular feelings to get sb's attention or good opinion
get wised up (slang) to become informed
hooey ['hu:i] (slang) nonsense

loco ['ləʊkəʊ] (AE, slang) crazy
nuts (AE, slang) crazy, foolish

washed up (AE, slang) finished, done for

refined cultivated, elegant

no, siree, Bob [ˌsɜ:'ri:] (slang) most certainly not, no way

frolic have fun, to play about in a happy and carefree way
called on the carpet (AE) called to the office of sb in authority to be roundly criticized
squirm to wriggle, to move one's body in snake-like fashion; (here) to get out of

How fair is Stanley's judgement of Blanche? Does it tell the whole story? How do you explain Stanley's eagerness to find out everything about his sister-in-law?

the jig was all up (slang) it was all over
town ordinance ['ɔ:dɪnəns] (AE) a statute, regulation issued by a municipality (town)

STANLEY Honey, I told you I thoroughly checked on these stories! Now wait till I finished. The trouble with Dame Blanche was that she couldn't put on her act any more in Laurel! They got wised up after two or three dates with her and then they quit, and she goes on to another, the same old line, same old act, same old hooey! But the town was too small for this to go on forever! And as time went by she became a town character. Regarded as not just different but downright loco – nuts.

[*Stella draws back.*]

And for the last year or two she has been washed up like poison. That's why she's here this summer, visiting royalty, putting on all this act – because she's practically told by the mayor to get out of town! Yes, did you know there was an army camp near Laurel and your sister's was one of the places called "Out-of-Bounds"?

BLANCHE "It's only a paper moon,
Just as phony as it can be –
But it wouldn't be make-believe
If you believed in me!"

STANLEY Well, so much for her being such a refined and particular type of girl. Which brings us to Lie Number Two.

STELLA I don't want to hear any more!

STANLEY She's not going back to teach school! In fact I am willing to bet you that she never had no idea of returning to Laurel! She didn't resign temporarily from the high school because of her nerves! No, siree, Bob! She didn't. They kicked her out of that high school before the spring term ended – and I hate to tell you the reason that step was taken! A seventeen-year-old boy – she'd gotten mixed up with!

BLANCHE "It's a Barnum and Bailey world,
Just as phony as it can be –"

[*In the bathroom the water goes on loud; little breathless cries and peals of laughter are heard as if a child were frolicking in the tub.*]

STELLA This is making me – sick!

STANLEY The boy's dad learned about it and got in touch with the high school superintendent. Boy, oh, boy, I'd like to have been in that office when Dame Blanche was called on the carpet! I'd like to have seen her trying to squirm out of that one! But they had her on the hook good and proper that time and she knew that the jig was all up! They told her she better move on to some fresh territory. Yep, it was practickly a town ordinance passed against her!

[*The bathroom door is opened and Blanche thrusts her head out, holding a towel about her hair.*]

BLANCHE Stella!

STELLA [*faintly*] Yes, Blanche?

BLANCHE Give me another bath-towel to dry my hair with. I've just washed it.

STELLA Yes, Blanche.

[*She crosses in a dazed way from the kitchen to the bathroom door with a towel.*]

BLANCHE What's the matter, honey?

STELLA Matter? Why?

BLANCHE You have such a strange expression on your face!

STELLA Oh – [*She tries to laugh*] I guess I'm a little tired!

BLANCHE Why don't you bathe, too, soon as I get out?

STANLEY [*calling from the kitchen*] How soon is that going to be?

BLANCHE Not so terribly long! Possess your soul in patience!

STANLEY It's not my soul, it's my kidneys I'm worried about!

[*Blanche slams the door. Stanley laughs harshly. Stella comes slowly back into the kitchen.*]

STANLEY Well, what do you think of it?

STELLA I don't believe all of those stories and I think your supply-man was mean and rotten to tell them. It's possible that some of the things he said are partly true. There are things about my sister I don't approve of – things that caused sorrow at home. She was always – flighty!

STANLEY Flighty!

STELLA But when she was young, very young, she married a boy who wrote poetry ... He was extremely good-looking. I think Blanche didn't just love him but worshipped the ground he walked on! Adored him and thought him almost too fine to be human! But then she found out –

STANLEY What?

STELLA This beautiful and talented young man was a degenerate. Didn't your supply-man give you that information?

STANLEY All we discussed was recent history. That must have been a pretty long time ago.

STELLA Yes, it was – a pretty long time ago ...

[*Stanley comes up and takes her by the shoulders rather gently. She gently withdraws from him. Automatically she starts sticking little pink candles in the birthday cake.*]

STANLEY How many candles you putting in that cake?

STELLA I'll stop at twenty-five.

STANLEY Is company expected?

STELLA We asked Mitch to come over for cake and ice cream.

possess your soul in patience [pə'zes] (formal) be patient

mean and rotten small-minded, base, and disagreeable; malicious, ill-willed

flighty frivolous and irresponsible; changing one's opinions often and being interested only for a short time (of a woman)

worship to show religious devotion; to have intense love and admiration for

degenerate [dɪ'dʒenərət] sb who is morally corrupt; (here) homosexual

[Stanley looks a little uncomfortable. He lights a cigarette from the one he has just finished.]

STANLEY I wouldn't be expecting Mitch over tonight.

[Stella pauses in her occupation with candles and looks slowly around at Stanley.]

STELLA Why?

buddy (AE, informal) a close friend
outfit (AE) (here) a military unit

STANLEY Mitch is a buddy of mine. We were in the same outfit together – Two-forty-first Engineers. We work in the same plant and now on the same bowling team. You think I could face him if –

STELLA Stanley Kowalski, did you – did you repeat what that –?

What do you think of Stanley's telling Mitch about his discoveries? Do you believe him when he advances his friendship for Mitch as the main reason for telling him?

STANLEY You're goddam right I told him! I'd have that on my conscience the rest of my life if I knew all that stuff and let my best friend get caught!

STELLA Is Mitch through with her?

STANLEY Wouldn't you be if –?

STELLA I said, *Is Mitch through with her?*

[Blanche's voice is lifted again, serenely as a bell. She sings "But it wouldn't be make-believe if you believed in me."]

STANLEY No, I don't think he's necessarily through with her – just wised up!

STELLA Stanley, she thought Mitch was – going to – going to marry her. I was hoping so, too.

tank water tank
school of sharks *ein Schwarm von Haien*

STANLEY Well, he's not going to marry her. Maybe he *was*, but he's not going to jump in a tank with a school of sharks – now! [*He rises*] Blanche! Oh, Blanche! Can I please get in my bathroom? [*There is a pause.*]

BLANCHE Yes, indeed, sir! Can you wait one second while I dry?

STANLEY Having waited one hour I guess one second ought to pass in a hurry.

STELLA And she hasn't got her job? Well, what will she do!

STANLEY She's not stayin' here after Tuesday. You know that, don't you? Just to make sure I bought her ticket myself. A bus-ticket!

STELLA In the first place, Blanche wouldn't go on a bus.

STANLEY She'll go on a bus and like it.

STELLA No, she won't, no, she won't, Stanley!

period an exclamation used to say that no further discussion will be allowed ("period" is AE for BE "full stop")
mapped out arranged, planned in detail

STANLEY *She'll go!* Period. P.S. She'll go *Tuesday!*

STELLA [*slowly*] What'll – she – do? What on earth will she – *do*!

STANLEY Her future is mapped out for her.

STELLA What do you mean?

[Blanche sings.]

toots (slang, now dated) darling

STANLEY Hey, canary bird! Toots! Get *OUT* of the *BATHROOM!*

[*The bathroom door flies open and Blanche emerges with a gay peal of laughter, but as Stanley crosses past her, a frightened look appears on her face, almost a look of panic. He doesn't look at her but slams the bathroom door shut as he goes in.*]

Blanche [*snatching up a hair-brush*] Oh, I feel so good after my long, hot bath, I feel so good and cool and – rested!

Stella [*sadly and doubtfully from the kitchen*] Do you, Blanche?

Blanche [*brushing her hair vigorously*] Yes, I do, so refreshed! [*She tinkles her highball glass.*] A hot bath and a long, cold drink always give me a brand new outlook on life! [*She looks through the portieres at Stella, standing between them, and slowly stops brushing*] Something has happened! – What is it?

Stella [*turning away quickly*] Why, nothing has happened, Blanche.

Blanche You're lying! Something has!

[*She stares fearfully at Stella, who pretends to be busy at the table. The distant piano goes into a hectic breakdown.*]

emerge come into view, appear

vigorous strong, forceful

tinkle to make light ringing sounds (like a bell or ice-cubes in a glass)

highball (AE) whiskey or brandy mixed with water or soda and served with ice in a tall glass

breakdown (AE) a lively country dance; also a sudden mental collapse

A band performing at Preservation Hall, New Orleans

Scene Eight

torch burning material that produces light at one end (*Fackel*)
oil-drum a large, round container for storing oil
pierce to make a hole in or through sth
sullen unsociable, withdrawn, angry and silent

Three-quarters of an hour later.

The view through the big windows is fading gradually into a still-golden dusk. A torch of sunlight blazes on the side of a big water-tank or oil-drum across the empty lot toward the business district which is now pierced by pinpoints of lighted windows or windows reflecting the sunset.

The three people are completing a dismal birthday supper. Stanley looks sullen. Stella is embarrassed and sad.

Blanche has a tight, artificial smile on her drawn face. There is a fourth place at the table which is left vacant.

stand sb up (informal) to fail to appear at a pre-arranged meeting
beau [bəʊ] (old-fashioned) the sweetheart or courtier of a woman

BLANCHE [*suddenly*] Stanley, tell us a joke, tell us a funny story to make us all laugh. I don't know what's the matter, we're all so solemn. Is it because I've been stood up by my beau? [*Stella laughs feebly.*]
It's the first time in my entire experience with men, and I've had a good deal of all sorts, that I've actually been stood up by anybody! Ha-ha! I don't know how to take it ... Tell us a funny little story, Stanley! Something to help us out.

STANLEY I didn't think you liked my stories, Blanche.

BLANCHE I like them when they're amusing but not indecent.

STANLEY I don't know any refined enough for your taste.

BLANCHE Then let me tell one.

STELLA Yes, you tell one, Blanche. You used to know lots of good stories.
[*The music fades.*]

repertoire ['repətwa:] a stock of stories, songs, etc.
parrot *Papagei*

curse a blue streak to curse a lot in shocking language

BLANCHE Let me see, now ... I must run through my repertoire! Oh, yes – I love parrot stories! Do you all like parrot stories? Well, this one's about the old maid and the parrot. This old maid, she had a parrot that cursed a blue streak and knew more vulgar expressions than Mr. Kowalski!

STANLEY Huh.

BLANCHE And the only way to hush the parrot up was to put the cover back on its cage so it would think it was night and go back to sleep. Well, one morning the old maid had just uncovered the parrot for the day – when who should she see coming up the front walk but the preacher! Well, she rushed back to the parrot and slipped the cover back on the cage and then she let in the preacher. And the parrot was perfectly still, just as quiet as a mouse, but just as she was asking the preacher how much sugar he wanted in his coffee – the parrot broke the silence with a loud – [*She whistles*] – and said –"God *damn*, but that was a short day!"

[She throws back her head and laughs. Stella also makes an ineffectual effort to seem amused. Stanley pays no attention to the story but reaches way over the table to spear his fork into the remaining chop which he eats with his fingers.]

BLANCHE Apparently Mr. Kowalski was not amused.

STELLA Mr. Kowalski is too busy making a pig of himself to think of anything else!

STANLEY That's right, baby.

STELLA Your face and your fingers are disgustingly greasy. Go and wash up and then help me clear the table.

[*He hurls a plate to the floor.*]

Stanley starting to clear the table.
From Elia Kazan's film

STANLEY That's how I'll clear the table! [*He seizes her arm*] Don't ever talk that way to me! "Pig – Polack – disgusting – vulgar – greasy!" – them kind of words have been on your tongue and your sister's too much around here! What do you two think you are? A pair of queens? Remember what Huey Long said – "Every Man is a King!" And I am the king around here, so don't forget it! [*He hurls a cup and saucer to the floor*] My place is cleared! You want me to clear your places?

[*Stella begins to cry weakly. Stanley stalks out on the porch and lights a cigarette.*

[*The Negro entertainers around the corner are heard.*]

BLANCHE What happened while I was bathing? What did he tell you, Stella?

STELLA Nothing, nothing, nothing!

BLANCHE I think he told you something about Mitch and me! You know why Mitch didn't come but you won't tell me! [*Stella shakes her head helplessly*] I'm going to call him!

ineffectual [ˌɪnɪˈfektʃuəl] not producing the desired effect, weak and unsuccessful

chop *Kotelett*

make a pig of oneself to eat greedily and too much without caring about table manners

Huey Long influential Louisianan politician (1893–1935), who as governor and senator stood for anti-capitalistic ideas and ruled autocratically until his murder in 1935

stalk out to walk out stiffly and grimly

Magnolia 9047 telephone numbers in the USA used to be a combination of a name and a number (the magnolia is the state flower of Louisiana)

get the coloured lights going (here) to have sex

chuckle to laugh softly, as if in mild amusement

reflective thoughtful

STELLA I wouldn't call him, Blanche.

BLANCHE I am, I'm going to call him on the phone.

STELLA [*miserably*] I wish you wouldn't.

BLANCHE I intend to be given some explanation from someone! [*She rushes to the phone in the bedroom. Stella goes out on the porch and stares reproachfully at her husband. He grunts and turns away from her.*]

STELLA I hope you're pleased with your doings. I never had so much trouble swallowing food in my life, looking at that girl's face and the empty chair! [*She cries quietly.*]

BLANCHE [*at the phone*] Hello. Mr. Mitchell, please ... Oh ... I would like to leave a number if I may. Magnolia 9047. And say it's important to call ... Yes, very important ... Thank you. [*She remains by the phone with a lost, frightened look.*]

[*Stanley turns slowly back toward his wife and takes her clumsily in his arms.*]

STANLEY Stell, it's gonna be all right after she goes and after you've had the baby. It's gonna be all right again between you and me the way that it was. You remember that way that it was? Them nights we had together? God, honey, it's gonna be sweet when we can make noise in the night the way that we used to and get the colored lights going with nobody's sister behind the curtains to hear us!

[*Their upstairs neighbors are heard in bellowing laughter at something. Stanley chuckles.*]

Steve an' Eunice ...

STELLA Come on back in. [*She returns to the kitchen and starts lighting the candles on the white cake.*] Blanche?

BLANCHE Yes. [*She returns from the bedroom to the table in the kitchen.*] Oh, those pretty little candles! Oh, don't burn them, Stella.

STELLA I certainly will.

[*Stanley comes back in.*]

BLANCHE You ought to save them for baby's birthdays. Oh, I hope candles are going to glow in his life and I hope that his eyes are going to be like candles, like two blue candles lighted in a white cake!

STANLEY [*sitting down*] What poetry!

BLANCHE [*she pauses reflectively for a moment*] I shouldn't have called him.

STELLA There's lots of things could have happened.

BLANCHE There's no excuse for it, Stella. I don't have to put up with insults. I won't be taken for granted.

STANLEY Goddamn, it's hot in here with the steam from the bathroom.

BLANCHE I've said I was sorry three times. [*The piano fades out.*] I take hot baths for my nerves. Hydro-therapy, they call it. You healthy Polack, without a nerve in your body, of course you don't know what anxiety feels like!

STANLEY I am not a Polack. People from Poland are Poles, not Polacks. But what I am is a one hundred percent American, born and raised in the greatest country on earth and proud as hell of it, so don't ever call me a Polack.

[*The phone rings. Blanche rises expectantly.*]

BLANCHE Oh, that's for me, I'm sure.

STANLEY *I'm* not sure. Keep your seat. [*He crosses leisurely to phone.*] H'lo. Aw, yeh, hello, Mac.

[*He leans against wall, staring insultingly in at Blanche. She sinks back in her chair with a frightened look. Stella leans over and touches her shoulder.*]

BLANCHE Oh, keep your hands on me, Stella. What is the matter with you? Why do you look at me with that pitying look?

STANLEY [*bawling*] QUIET IN THERE! – We've got a noisy woman on the place. – Go on, Mac. At Riley's? No, I don't wanta bowl at Riley's. I had a little trouble with Riley last week. I'm the team-captain, ain't I? All right, then, we're not gonna bowl at Riley's, we're gonna bowl at the West Side or the Gala! All right, Mac. See you!

[*He hangs up and returns to the table. Blanche fiercely controls herself, drinking quickly from her tumbler of water. He doesn't look at her but reaches in a pocket. Then he speaks slowly and with false amiability.*]

Sister Blanche, I've got a little birthday remembrance for you.

BLANCHE Oh, have you, Stanley? I wasn't expecting any, I – I don't know why Stella wants to observe my birthday! I'd much rather forget it – when you – reach twenty-seven! Well – age is a subject that you'd prefer to – ignore!

STANLEY Twenty-seven?

BLANCHE [*quickly*] What is it? Is it for me?

[*He is holding a little envelope toward her.*]

STANLEY Yes, I hope you like it!

BLANCHE Why, why – Why, it's a –

STANLEY Ticket! Back to Laurel! On the Greyhound! Tuesday!

[*The Varsouviana music steals in softly and continues playing. Stella rises abruptly and turns her back. Blanche tries to smile. Then she tries to laugh. Then she gives both up and springs from the table and runs into the next room. She clutches her throat and then runs into the bathroom. Coughing, gagging sounds are heard.*]

Well!

hydro-therapy [ˌhaɪdrəʊˈθerəpi] the treatment of a disease by the use of water

Why does Stanley insist that he is a genuine American?

amiability [ˌeɪmiəˈbɪləti] friendliness

Greyhound a bus company in the USA that operates long-distance travel

What do you think of the methods Stanley uses to get rid of Blanche? Look at Stanley's speeches to Stella on p. 72 and p. 74.

gag to retch or choke (*würgen*)

STELLA You didn't need to do that.

STANLEY Don't forget all that I took off her.

STELLA You needn't have been so cruel to someone alone as she is.

STANLEY Delicate piece she is.

STELLA She is. She was. You didn't know Blanche as a girl. Nobody, nobody, was tender and trusting as she was. But people like you abused her, and forced her to change.

abuse [ə'bju:z] to use wrongly, to treat badly

[He crosses into the bedroom, ripping off his shirt, and changes into a brilliant silk bowling shirt. She follows him.]

Do you think you're going bowling now?

STANLEY Sure.

STELLA You're not going bowling. [*She catches hold of his shirt*] Why did you do this to her?

STANLEY I done nothing to no one. Let go of my shirt. You've torn it.

STELLA I want to know why. Tell me why.

STANLEY When we first met, me and you, you thought I was common. How right you was, baby. I was common as dirt. You showed me the snapshot of the place with the columns. I pulled you down off them columns and how you loved it, having them colored lights going! And wasn't we happy together, wasn't it all okay till she showed here?

[Stella makes a slight movement. Her look goes suddenly inward as if some interior voice had called her name. She begins a slow, shuffling progress from the bedroom to the kitchen, leaning and resting on the back of the chair and then on the edge of a table with a blind look and listening expression. Stanley, finishing with his shirt, is unaware of her reaction.]

And wasn't we happy together? Wasn't it all okay? Till she showed here. Hoity-toity, describing me as an ape. [*He suddenly notices the change in Stella*] Hey, what is it, Stell? [*He crosses to her.*]

hoity-toity arrogant, haughty

STELLA [*quietly*] Take me to the hospital.

[He is with her now, supporting her with his arm, murmuring indistinguishably as they go outside.]

Scene Nine

A while later that evening. Blanche is seated in a tense hunched position in a bedroom chair that she has recovered with diagonal green and white stripes. She has on her scarlet satin robe. On the table beside chair is a bottle of liquor and a glass. The rapid, feverish polka tune, the "Varsouviana," is heard. The music is in her mind; she is drinking to escape it and the sense of disaster closing in on her, and she seems to whisper the words of the song. An electric fan is turning back and forth across her.

Mitch comes around the corner in work clothes: blue denim shirt and pants. He is unshaven. He climbs the steps to the door and rings. Blanche is startled.

BLANCHE Who is it, please?

MITCH [*hoarsely*] Me. Mitch.

[*The polka tune stops.*]

BLANCHE Mitch! – Just a minute.

[*She rushes about frantically, hiding the bottle in a closet, crouching at the mirror and dabbing her face with cologne and powder. She is so excited that her breath is audible as she dashes about. At last she rushes to the door in the kitchen and lets him in.*]

Mitch! – Y'know, I really shouldn't let you in after the treatment I have received from you this evening! So utterly uncavalier! But hello, beautiful!

[*She offers him her lips. He ignores it and pushes past her into the flat. She looks fearfully after him as he stalks into the bedroom.*]

My, my, what a cold shoulder! And such uncouth apparel! Why, you haven't even shaved! The unforgivable insult to a lady! But I forgive you. I forgive you because it's such a relief to see you. You've stopped that polka tune that I had caught in my head. Have you ever had anything caught in your head? No, of course you haven't, you dumb angel-puss, you'd never get anything awful caught in your head!

[*He stares at her while she follows him while she talks. It is obvious that he has had a few drinks on the way over.*]

MITCH Do we have to have that fan on?

BLANCHE No!

MITCH I don't like fans.

BLANCHE Then let's turn it off, honey. I'm not partial to them!

[*She presses the switch and the fan nods slowly off. She clears her throat uneasily as Mitch plumps himself down on the bed in the bedroom and lights a cigarette.*]

I don't know what there is to drink. I – haven't investigated.

MITCH I don't want Stan's liquor.

tense showing mental strain, anxious, strained, nervous
hunched sitting or standing with one's back arched; bent forward

Again, these stage directions contain elements that can-not be put on stage directly. What are they? What can a director do to at least suggest these elements?

close in on to move closer in a threatening way, ready to attack

hoarse (voice) harsh and grating, sounding rough

frantic done in a quick and desperate way because one is about to panic
dab to touch lightly and quickly
audible loud enough to be heard
dash about to move about quickly
uncavalier [ˌʌnkævəˈlɪə] not like a gentleman

uncouth [ʌnˈkuːθ] clumsy, boorish, uncultured
apparel [əˈpærəl] clothing

angel-puss [pʊs] (slang) angel face

partial to fond of

plump oneself down on to drop down heavily on

premises ['premɪsɪz] a building and its land

cross-examine to question a witness so as to challenge their truthfulness

boxed out of your mind (slang) completely crazy

Southern Comfort a brand of a strong sweet alcoholic drink based on whiskey

liqueur [lɪ'kjʊə] a strong, sweet alcoholic drink (don't confuse with "liquor": any alcoholic drink)

lay off (informal) to stop using

lap it up (informal) to drink greedily and in huge quantities

BLANCHE It isn't Stan's. Everything here isn't Stan's. Some things on the premises are actually mine! How is your mother? Isn't your mother well?

MITCH Why?

BLANCHE Something's the matter tonight, but never mind. I won't cross-examine the witness. I'll just – [*She touches her forehead vaguely. The polka tune starts up again.*] – pretend I don't notice anything different about you! That – music again ...

MITCH What music?

BLANCHE The "Varsouviana"! The polka tune they were playing when Allan – Wait!
[*A distant revolver shot is heard. Blanche seems relieved.*]
There now, the shot! It always stops after that.
[*The polka music dies out again.*]
Yes, now it's stopped.

MITCH Are you boxed out of your mind?

BLANCHE I'll go and see what I can find in the way of – [*She crosses into the closet, pretending to search for the bottle.*]
Oh, by the way, excuse me for not being dressed. But I'd practically given you up! Had you forgotten your invitation to supper?

MITCH I wasn't going to see you any more.

BLANCHE Wait a minute. I can't hear what you're saying and you talk so little that when you do say something, I don't want to miss a single syllable of it ... What am I looking around here for? Oh, yes – liquor! We've had so much excitement around here this evening that I *am* boxed out of my mind! [*She pretends suddenly to find the bottle. He draws his foot up on the bed and stares at her contemptuously.*] Here's something. Southern Comfort! What is that, I wonder?

MITCH If you don't know, it must belong to Stan.

BLANCHE Take your foot off the bed. It has a light cover on it. Of course you boys don't notice things like that. I've done so much with this place since I've been here.

MITCH I bet you have.

BLANCHE You saw it before I came. Well, look at it now! This room is almost – dainty! I want to keep it that way. I wonder if this stuff ought to be mixed with something? Ummm, it's sweet, so sweet! It's terribly, terribly sweet!
Why, it's a *liqueur*, I believe! Yes, that's what it *is*, a liqueur! [*Mitch grunts.*] I'm afraid you won't like it, but try it, and maybe you will.

MITCH I told you already I don't want none of his liquor and I mean it. You ought to lay off his liquor. He says you been lapping it up all summer like a wildcat!

BLANCHE What a fantastic statement! Fantastic of him to say it, fantastic of you to repeat it! I won't descend to the level of such cheap accusations to answer them, even!

MITCH Huh.

BLANCHE What's in your mind? I see something in your eyes!

MITCH [*getting up*] It's dark in here.

BLANCHE I like it dark. The dark is comforting to me.

MITCH I don't think I ever seen you in the light. [*Blanche laughs breathlessly*] That's a fact!

BLANCHE Is it?

MITCH I've never seen you in the afternoon.

BLANCHE Whose fault is that?

MITCH You never want to go out in the afternoon.

BLANCHE Why, Mitch, you're at the plant in the afternoon!

MITCH Not Sunday afternoon. I've asked you to go out with me sometimes on Sundays but you always make an excuse. You never want to go out till after six and then it's always some place that's not lighted much.

BLANCHE There is some obscure meaning in this but I fail to catch it.

MITCH What it means is I've never had a real good look at you, Blanche. Let's turn the light on here.

BLANCHE [*fearfully*] Light? Which light? What for?

MITCH This one with the paper thing on it. [*He tears the paper lantern off the light bulb. She utters a frightened gasp.*]

BLANCHE What did you do that for?

MITCH So I can take a look at you good and plain!

BLANCHE Of course you don't really mean to be insulting!

fantastic strange and unusual, eccentric
descend (here) to lower oneself, to stoop, to do sth that you think is beneath you

obscure [əb'skjʊə] not clear or distinct, not easily understood

gasp quick, deep breath

"I've never had a real good look at you …"
From Elia Kazan's film

misrepresent to represent falsely, to give a wrong idea of

pitch (slang) sb's line of talk (especially the talk a salesman uses)
malarkey (slang) insincere, deliberately misleading talk
dish out to tell untrue stories about sth
straight honest, decent

long-distance (telephone) *Ferngespräch*

put sb in his/her place to show sb who is arrogant and overconfident that they overestimate themselves

rub-a-dub-dub the beginning of a nursery rhyme
tub a round, open container, often used for taking a bath
tarantula [təˈræntʃələ] poisonous spider (*Tarantel*)
arms the insignia of a country, a guild, etc. (coat of arms)

convulsive [kənˈvʌlsɪv] having involuntary contractions (spasms) of the muscles

MITCH No, just realistic.

BLANCHE I don't want realism. I want magic! [*Mitch laughs*] Yes, yes, magic! I try to give that to people. I misrepresent things to them. I don't tell truth, I tell what *ought* to be truth. And if that is sinful, then let me be damned for it! – Don't turn the light on!

[*Mitch crosses to the switch. He turns the light on and stares at her. She cries out and covers her face. He turns the light off again.*]

MITCH [*slowly and bitterly*] I don't mind you being older than what I thought. But all the rest of it – Christ! That pitch about your ideals being so old-fashioned and all the malarkey that you've dished out all summer. Oh, I knew you weren't sixteen any more. But I was a fool enough to believe you was straight.

BLANCHE Who told you I wasn't – 'straight'? My loving brother-in-law. And you believed him.

MITCH I called him a liar at first. And then I checked on the story. First I asked our supply-man who travels through Laurel. And then I talked directly over long-distance to this merchant.

BLANCHE Who is this merchant?

MITCH Kiefaber.

BLANCHE The merchant Kiefaber of Laurel! I know the man. He whistled at me. I put him in his place. So now for revenge he makes up stories about me.

MITCH Three people, Kiefaber, Stanley and Shaw, swore to them!

BLANCHE Rub-a-dub-dub, three men in a tub! And such a filthy tub!

MITCH Didn't you stay at a hotel called the Flamingo?

BLANCHE Flamingo? No! Tarantula was the name of it! I stayed at a hotel called the Tarantula Arms!

MITCH [*stupidly*] Tarantula?

BLANCHE Yes, a big spider! That's where I brought my victims. [*She pours herself another drink*] Yes, I had many intimacies with strangers. After the death of Allan – intimacies with strangers was all I seemed able to fill my empty heart with ... I think it was panic, just panic, that drove me from one to another, hunting for some protection – here and there, in the most – unlikely places – even, at last, in a seventeen-year-old boy but – somebody wrote the superintendent about it – "This woman is morally unfit for her position!" [*She throws back her head with convulsive, sobbing laughter. Then she repeats the statement, gasps, and drinks.*]

True? Yes, I suppose – unfit somehow – anyway ... So I came here. There was nowhere else I could go. I was played out. You know what played out is? My youth was suddenly gone up the water-spout, and – I met you. You said you needed somebody. Well, I needed somebody, too. I thanked God for you, because you seemed to be gentle – a cleft in the rock of the world that I could hide in! But I guess I was asking, hoping – too much! Kiefaber, Stanley and Shaw have tied an old tin can to the tail of the kite.

[*There is a pause. Mitch stares at her dumbly.*]

MITCH You lied to me, Blanche.

BLANCHE Don't say I lied to you.

MITCH Lies, lies, inside and out, all lies.

BLANCHE Never inside, I didn't lie in my heart ...

[*A Vendor comes around the corner. She is a blind Mexican woman in a dark shawl, carrying bunches of those gaudy tin flowers that lower class Mexicans display at funerals and other festive occasions. She is calling barely audibly. Her figure is only faintly visible outside the building.*]

MEXICAN WOMAN Flores. Flores. Flores para los muertos. Flores. Flores.

BLANCHE What? Oh! Somebody outside ... [*She goes to the door, opens it and stares at the Mexican Woman.*]

MEXICAN WOMAN [*she is at the door and offers Blanche some of her flowers*] Flores? Flores para los muertos?

"Flores para los muertos." From Elia Kazan's film

BLANCHE [*frightened*] No, no! Not now! Not now!

[*She darts back into the apartment, slamming the door.*]

MEXICAN WOMAN [*she turns away and starts to move down the street*] Flores para los muertos.

[*The polka tune fades in.*]

BLANCHE [*as if to herself*] Crumble and fade and – regrets –

played out exhausted, having no energy

go up in a water-spout disappear (a reference to a nursery rhyme in which a spider climbs up a water spout)

cleft a crack, a hollow in the surface of rocks

Is Blanche justified in saying, "Never inside, I didn't lie in my heart ..."?

shawl square piece of cloth, worn by women, as a covering for the head or shoulders (Careful! The German word "*Schal*" is "scarf" in English.)

flores para los muertos (Spanish) flowers for the dead

crumble to fall to pieces, to disintegrate

recrimination an accusation, a reproach

corones (Spanish) crown

legacy the money or property left to sb by a will; anything handed down from an ancestor

pillow-slip a pillowcase (*Kopfkissenbezug*)

recriminations ... 'If you'd done this, it wouldn't've cost me that!'

MEXICAN WOMAN Corones para los muertos. Corones ...

BLANCHE Legacies! Huh ... And other things such as blood-stained pillow-slips – 'Her linen needs changing' – 'Yes Mother. But couldn't we get a colored girl to do it?' No, we couldn't of course. Everything gone but the –

MEXICAN WOMAN Flores.

BLANCHE Death – I used to sit here and she used to sit over there and death was as close as you are ... We didn't dare even admit we had ever heard of it!

MEXICAN WOMAN Flores para los muertos, flores – flores ...

BLANCHE The opposite is desire. So do you wonder? How could you possibly wonder! Not far from Belle Reve, before we had lost Belle Reve, was a camp where they trained young soldiers. On Saturday nights they would go in town to get drunk –

MEXICAN WOMAN [*softly*] Corones ...

stagger to walk unsteadily

BLANCHE – and on the way back they would stagger onto my lawn and call – 'Blanche! Blanche!' – The deaf old lady remaining suspected nothing. But sometimes I slipped outside to answer their calls ... Later the paddy-wagon would gather them up like daisies ... the long way home ...

paddy-wagon (slang) a patrol car, a police car used to patrol an area or to transport prisoners

mournful sad, melancholy

purposeful having a clear aim and pursuing it resolutely

[*The Mexican Woman turns slowly and drifts back off with her soft mournful cries. Blanche goes to the dresser and leans forward on it. After a moment, Mitch rises and follows her purposefully. The polka music fades away. He places his hands on her waist and tries to turn her about.*]

BLANCHE What do you want?

fumble to search or try to hold by feeling about awkwardly with your hands

MITCH [*fumbling to embrace her*] What I been missing all summer.

BLANCHE Then marry me, Mitch!

MITCH I don't think I want to marry you any more.

BLANCHE No?

Does this scene change your ➔ picture of Mitch? Can you understand his conduct?

MITCH [*dropping his hands from her waist*] You're not clean enough to bring in the house with my mother.

BLANCHE Go away, then. [*He stares at her*] Get out of here quick before I start screaming fire! [*Her throat is tightening with hysteria*] Get out of here quick before I start screaming fire. [*He still remains staring. She suddenly rushes to the big window with its pale blue square of the soft summer light and cries wildly.*] Fire! Fire! Fire!

clatter to move with a succession of loud, sharp noises

[*With a startled gasp, Mitch turns and goes out the outer door, clatters awkwardly down the steps and around the corner of the building. Blanche staggers back from the window and falls to her knees. The distant piano is slow and blue.*]

Scene Ten

It is a few hours later that night.

Blanche has been drinking fairly steadily since Mitch left. She has dragged her wardrobe trunk into the center of the bedroom. It hangs open with flowery dresses thrown across it. As the drinking and packing went on, a mood of hysterical exhilaration came into her and she has decked herself out in a somewhat soiled and crumpled white satin evening gown and a pair of scuffed silver slippers with brilliants set in their heels.

Now she is placing the rhinestone tiara on her head before the mirror of the dressing-table and murmuring excitedly as if to a group of spectral admirers.

BLANCHE How about taking a swim, a moonlight swim at the old rock-quarry? If anyone's sober enough to drive a car! Ha-ha! Best way in the world to stop your head buzzing! Only you've got to be careful to dive where the deep pool is – if you hit a rock you don't come up till tomorrow ...

[*Tremblingly she lifts the hand mirror for a closer inspection. She catches her breath and slams the mirror face down with such violence that the glass cracks. She moans a little and attempts to rise.*

Stanley appears around the corner of the building. He still has on the vivid green silk bowling shirt. As he rounds the corner the honky-tonk music is heard. It continues softly throughout the scene.

He enters the kitchen, slamming the door. As he peers in at Blanche, he gives a low whistle. He has had a few drinks on the way and has brought some quart beer bottles home with him.]

BLANCHE How is my sister?

STANLEY She is doing okay.

BLANCHE And how is the baby?

STANLEY [*grinning amiably*] The baby won't come before morning so they told me to go home and get a little shut-eye.

BLANCHE Does that mean we are to be alone in here?

STANLEY Yep. Just me and you, Blanche. Unless you got somebody hid under the bed. What've you got on those fine feathers for?

BLANCHE Oh, that's right. You left before my wire came.

STANLEY You got a wire?

BLANCHE I received a telegram from an old admirer of mine.

STANLEY Anything good?

BLANCHE I think so. An invitation.

STANLEY What to? A fireman's ball?

➜ Read this scene in connection with the preceding one and contrast Mitch's and Stanley's behaviour. Think in terms of dramatic conventions like juxtaposition, similarity and contrast, gradation and climax as well as foreshadowing.

exhilaration [ɪgˌzɪlə'reɪʃn] high spirits, cheerfulness
deck out to decorate with flowers or ornaments
soiled dirty
crumpled crushed together so as to look untidy, creased
scuffed (shoes) worn out
slippers (here) high-heeled shoes
spectral like a ghost
rock-quarry ['kwɒri] a place where large amounts of stone can be dug out
peer in to look closely so as to see more clearly
quart (liquid measure) one fourth of a gallon (0.9464 litre)
shut-eye (informal) sleep
fine feathers (informal) fine clothes
fireman's ball a ball, entertainment organised by the local fire brigade

cruise a holiday voyage on a large ship
Caribbean [ˌkærə'biːən] a part of the Atlantic, bounded by the West Indies and Central America
yacht [jɒt] a boat for pleasure cruises
What do you know? Who would have expected that?
like a bolt from the blue all of a sudden, like a thunderbolt from a clear sky
ATO pin a membership pin of the Alpha Tau Omega fraternity (at a university)
Tiffany a valuable and stylish jewel (named for the American jeweller C.L. Tiffany, 1812–1902)
sack a brown bag used to wrap alcoholic drinks in
pound to hit hard
accomplishment [ə'kʌmplɪʃmənt] skill, ability
sneak to move quietly so as to avoid being seen or heard
geyser ['giːzə] AE ['gaɪzə] column of boiling water and steam

BLANCHE [*throwing back her head*] A cruise of the Caribbean on a yacht!

STANLEY Well, well. What do you know?

BLANCHE I have never been so surprised in my life.

STANLEY I guess not.

BLANCHE It came like a bolt from the blue!

STANLEY Who did you say it was from?

BLANCHE An old beau of mine.

STANLEY The one that give you the white fox-pieces?

BLANCHE Mr. Shep Huntleigh. I wore his ATO pin my last year at college. I hadn't seen him again until last Christmas. I ran into him on Biscayne Boulevard. Then – just now – this wire – inviting me on a cruise of the Caribbean! The problem is clothes. I tore into my trunk to see what I have that's suitable for the tropics!

STANLEY And come up with that – gorgeous – diamond – tiara?

BLANCHE This old relic? Ha-ha! It's only rhinestones.

STANLEY Gosh. I thought it was Tiffany diamonds. [*He unbuttons his shirt.*]

BLANCHE Well, anyhow, I shall be entertained in style.

STANLEY Uh-huh. It goes to show, you never know what is coming.

BLANCHE Just when I thought my luck had begun to fail me –

STANLEY Into the picture pops this Miami millionaire.

BLANCHE This man is not from Miami. This man is from Dallas.

STANLEY This man is from Dallas?

BLANCHE Yes, this man is from Dallas where gold spouts out of the ground!

STANLEY Well, just so he's from somewhere! [*He starts removing his shirt.*]

BLANCHE Close the curtains before you undress any further.

STANLEY [*amiably*] This is all I'm going to undress right now. [*He rips the sack off a quart beer-bottle*] Seen a bottle opener? [*She moves slowly toward the dresser, where she stands with her hands knotted together.*]
I used to have a cousin who could open a beer bottle with his teeth. [*Pounding the bottle cap on the corner of table*] That was his only accomplishment, all he could do – he was just a human bottle-opener. And then one time, at a wedding party, he broke his front teeth off! After that he was so ashamed of himself he used t' sneak out of the house when company came ...
[*The bottle cap pops off and a geyser of foam shoots up. Stanley laughs happily, holding up the bottle over his head.*]

Ha-ha! Rain from heaven! [*He extends the bottle toward her*] Shall we bury the hatchet and make it a loving-cup? Huh?

BLANCHE No, thank you.

STANLEY Well, it's a red letter night for us both. You having an oil-millionaire and me having a baby.

[*He goes to the bureau in the bedroom and crouches to remove something from the bottom drawer.*]

BLANCHE [*drawing back*] What are you doing in here?

STANLEY Here's something I always break out on special occasions like this. The silk pyjamas I wore on my wedding night!

BLANCHE Oh.

STANLEY When the telephone rings and they say, "You've got a son!" I'll tear this off and wave it like a flag! [*He shakes out a brilliant pyjama coat*] I guess we are both entitled to put on the dog. [*He goes back to the kitchen with the coat over his arm.*]

BLANCHE When I think of how divine it is going to be to have such a thing as privacy once more – I could weep with joy!

STANLEY This millionaire from Dallas is not going to interfere with your privacy any?

BLANCHE It won't be the sort of thing you have in mind. This man is a gentleman and he respects me. [*Improvising feverishly*] What he wants is my companionship. Having great wealth sometimes makes people lonely! A cultivated woman, a woman of intelligence and breeding, can enrich a man's life – immeasurably! I have those things to offer, and this doesn't take them away. Physical beauty is passing. A transitory possession. But beauty of the mind and richness of the spirit and tenderness of the heart – and I have all of those things – aren't taken away, but grow! Increase with the years! How strange that I should be called a destitute woman! When I have all of these treasures locked in my heart. [*A choked sob comes from her*] I think of myself as a very, very rich woman! But I have been foolish – casting my pearls before swine!

STANLEY Swine, huh?

BLANCHE Yes, swine! Swine! And I'm thinking not only of you but of your friend, Mr. Mitchell. He came to see me tonight. He dared to come here in his work-clothes! And to repeat slander to me, vicious stories that he had gotten from you! I gave him his walking papers ...

STANLEY You did, huh?

BLANCHE But then he came back. He returned with a box of roses to beg my forgiveness! He implored my forgiveness. But some things are not forgivable. Deliberate cruelty is not

bury the hatchet to make peace, to stop fighting
loving-cup at a feast or banquet, a cup passed from guest to guest
red letter night a memorable night, a night to celebrate (more often, a red-letter day)
crouch to bend low with the limbs drawn close to the body
break out (informal) to bring out for use

put on the dog (slang) to put on one's best clothes to make a show of being wealthy
divine [dɪ'vaɪn] (informal) great, pleasant (literally, "divine" is god-like or holy)

➊ What is Blanche's credo? Does it tally with her preceding statements (for instance, p. 52)?

breeding good upbringing and good education
immeasurable [ɪ'meʒərəbl] too large to be measured
transitory ['trænsətri] lasting only for a short time

destitute ['destɪtjuːt] living in complete poverty
cast one's pearls before swine (Biblical) to waste one's gifts or talents on people who are unable to value or appreciate them
slander false statement that is spoken in the presence of others meant to damage another person's reputation
vicious ['vɪʃəs] harmful and mean
give sb their walking papers (AE, informal) to tell sb that they have to leave, to dismiss
implore to ask or beg earnestly
deliberate [dɪ'lɪbərət] done on purpose, carefully thought out

Relate Blanche's belief that "deliberate cruelty is not forgivable" to Stanley's actions and words (previously and in the following passages). In this context, do her words also refer to Mitch? What about her own conduct with respect to her husband?

incompatible [ˌɪnkəmˈpætəbl] not able to exist in harmony; not getting along well together

conceit [kənˈsiːt] exaggerated opinion of oneself and one's merits, vanity

Mardi Gras [ˌmɑːdiˈgrɑː] (literally, Fat Tuesday) Shrove Tuesday, the last day before Lent beginning on Ash Wednesday; in New Orleans, a day of merrymaking and the climax of the carnival period

rag-picker sb who makes his or her living by picking up rags and junk to sell them (*Lumpensammler*)

be on to sb to see through sb

lo and behold (humorous), used before mentioning sth surprising

Queen of the Nile a reference to Cleopatra [ˌkliːəˈpætrə] the famous Queen of Egypt (c. 69–30 B.C.)

menacing [ˈmenəsɪŋ] threatening

jiggle the hook to move in quick jerks (formerly, telephone receivers hung on a hook)

forgivable. It is the one unforgivable thing in my opinion and it is the one thing of which I have never, never been guilty. And so I told him, I said to him, "Thank you," but it was foolish of me to think that we could ever adapt ourselves to each other. Our ways of life are too different. Our attitudes and our backgrounds are incompatible. We have to be realistic about such things. So farewell, my friend! And let there be no hard feelings ...

STANLEY Was this before or after the telegram came from the Texas oil millionaire?

BLANCHE What telegram? No! No, after! As a matter of fact, the wire came just as –

STANLEY As a matter of fact there wasn't no wire at all!

BLANCHE Oh, oh!

STANLEY There isn't no millionaire! And Mitch didn't come back with roses 'cause I know where he is –

BLANCHE Oh!

STANLEY There isn't a goddam thing but imagination!

BLANCHE Oh!

STANLEY And lies and conceit and tricks!

BLANCHE Oh!

STANLEY And look at yourself! Take a look at yourself in that worn-out Mardi Gras outfit, rented for fifty cents from some rag-picker! And with the crazy crown on! What queen do you think you are?

BLANCHE Oh – God ...

STANLEY I've been on to you from the start! Not once did you pull any wool over this boy's eyes! You come in here and sprinkle the place with powder and spray perfume and cover the light-bulb with a paper lantern, and lo and behold the place has turned into Egypt and you are the Queen of the Nile! Sitting on your throne and swilling down my liquor! I say – *Ha! – Ha!* Do you hear me? *Ha – ha – ha!* [*He walks into the bedroom.*]

BLANCHE Don't come in here!

[*Lurid reflections appear on the walls around Blanche. The shadows are of a grotesque and menacing form. She catches her breath, crosses to the phone and jiggles the hook. Stanley goes into the bathroom and closes the door.*]

Operator, operator! Give me long-distance, please ... I want to get in touch with Mr. Shep Huntleigh of Dallas. He's so well-known he doesn't require any address. Just ask anybody who – Wait!! – No, I couldn't find it right now ... Please understand, I – No! No, wait! ... One moment! Someone is – Nothing! Hold on, please!

[She sets the phone down and crosses warily into the kitchen. The night is filled with inhuman voices like cries in a jungle. The shadows and lurid reflections move sinuously as flames along the wall spaces.

Through the back wall of the rooms, which have become transparent, can be seen the sidewalk. A prostitute has rolled a drunkard. He pursues her along the walk, overtakes her and there is a struggle. A policeman's whistle breaks it up. The figures disappear. Some moments later the Negro Woman appears around the corner with a sequined bag which the prostitute had dropped on the walk. She is rooting excitedly through it.]

[Blanche presses her knuckles to her lips and returns slowly to the phone. She speaks in a hoarse whisper.]

BLANCHE Operator! Operator! Never mind long-distance. Get Western Union. There isn't time to be – Western – Western Union!

[She waits anxiously.]

Western Union? Yes! I – want to – Take down this message! "In desperate, desperate circumstances! Help me! Caught in a trap. Caught in –" *Oh!*

[The bathroom door is thrown open and STANLEY *comes out in the brilliant silk pyjamas. He grins at her as he knots the tasseled sash about his waist. She gasps and backs away from the phone. He stares at her for a count of ten. Then a clicking becomes audible from the telephone, steady and rasping.]*

STANLEY You left th' phone off th' hook.

[He crosses to it deliberately and sets it back on the hook. After he has replaced it, he stares at her again, his mouth slowly curving into a grin, as he weaves between Blanche and the outer door.]

[The barely audible "blue piano" begins to drum up louder. The sound of it turns into the roar of an approaching locomotive. Blanche crouches, pressing her fists to her ears until it has gone by.]

BLANCHE *[finally straightening]* Let me – let me get by you!

STANLEY Get by me! Sure. Go ahead. *[He moves back a pace in the doorway.]*

BLANCHE You – you stand over there! *[She indicates a further position.]*

STANLEY *[grinning]* You got plenty of room to walk by me now.

BLANCHE Not with you there! But I've got to get out somehow!

STANLEY You think I'll interfere with you? Ha-ha!

[The "blue piano" goes softly. She turns confusedly and makes a faint gesture. The inhuman jungle voices rise up. He takes a step toward her, biting his tongue which protrudes between his lips.]

wary [weəri] being on one's guard, cautious

sinuous ['sɪnjuəs] bending, curving, snake-like

transparent [træns'pærənt] capable of being seen through

roll (AE, slang) to rob sb who is drunk

sequined ['siːkwɪnd] decorated with small pieces of shiny metal

tasseled *mit Quasten oder Troddeln versehen*

sash an ornamental band or ribbon worn over the shoulder or around the waist

rasping in a rough, grating tone

➊ Is there a build-up to this scene in which Stanley is about to rape Blanche? Is there any excuse for Stanley's behaviour? Don't forget that he is a married man and a father as well.

get by sb to get past sb

protrude to stick or jut out

Stanley [*softly*] Come to think of it – maybe you wouldn't be bad to – interfere with ...

[*Blanche moves backward through the door into the bedroom.*]

Blanche Stay back! Don't you come toward me another step or I'll –

Stanley What?

Blanche Some awful thing will happen! It will!

put on (here) to produce sth that entertains people (a show, a party, etc.); to put on an act

Stanley What are you putting on now?

[*They are now both inside the bedroom.*]

Blanche I warn you, don't, I'm in danger!

[*He takes another step. She smashes a bottle on the table and faces him, clutching the broken top.*]

Stanley What did you do that for?

Blanche So I could twist the broken end in your face!

Stanley I bet you would do that!

Blanche I would! I will if you –

rough-house (informal) rough behaviour

Stanley Oh! So you want some rough-house! All right, let's have some rough-house!

[*He springs toward her, overturning the table. She cries out and strikes at him with the bottle top but he catches her wrist.*]

Tiger – tiger! Drop the bottle top! Drop it! We've had this date with each other from the beginning!

inert [ɪˈnɜːt] without power to move or resist

[*She moans. The bottle top falls. She sinks to her knees. He picks up her inert figure and carries her to the bed. The hot trumpet and drums from the Four Deuces sound loudly.*]

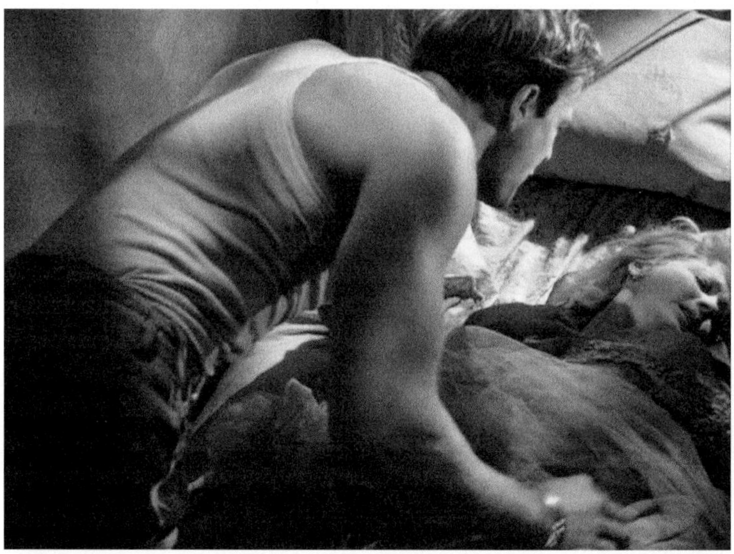

"We've had this date with each other from the beginning!" From Elia Kazan's film

Scene Eleven

It is some weeks later. Stella is packing Blanche's things. Sounds of water can be heard running in the bathroom.

The portieres are partly open on the poker players – Stanley, Steve, Mitch and Pablo – who sit around the table in the kitchen. The atmosphere of the kitchen is now the same raw, lurid one of the disastrous poker night.

The building is framed by the sky of turquoise. Stella has been crying as she arranges the flowery dresses in the open trunk.

Eunice comes down the steps from her flat above and enters the kitchen. There is an outburst from the poker table.

STANLEY Drew to an inside straight and made it, by God.

PABLO *Maldita sea tu suerto!*

STANLEY Put it in English, greaseball!

PABLO I am cursing your rutting luck.

STANLEY [*prodigiously elated*] You know what luck is? Luck is believing you're lucky. Take at Salerno. I believed I was lucky. I figured that 4 out of 5 would not come through but I would ... and I did. I put that down as a rule. To hold front position in this rat-race you've got to believe you are lucky.

MITCH You ... you ... you .... Brag ... brag ... bull ... bull.

[*Stella goes into the bedroom and starts folding a dress.*]

STANLEY What's the matter with him?

EUNICE [*walking past the table*] I always did say that men are callous things with no feelings, but this does beat anything. Making pigs of yourselves. [*She comes through the portieres into the bedroom.*]

STANLEY What's the matter with her?

STELLA How is my baby?

EUNICE Sleeping like a little angel. Brought you some grapes. [*She puts them on a stool and lowers her voice.*] Blanche?

STELLA Bathing.

EUNICE How is she?

STELLA She wouldn't eat anything but asked for a drink.

EUNICE What did you tell her?

STELLA I – just told her that – we'd made arrangements for her to rest in the country. She's got it mixed in her mind with Shep Huntleigh.

[*Blanche opens the bathroom door slightly.*]

BLANCHE Stella.

STELLA Yes, Blanche?

BLANCHE If anyone calls while I'm bathing take the number and tell them I'll call right back.

➊ The beginning of this scene seems to take up where Scene 3 left off. Is the atmosphere the same in the two scenes?

draw to an inside straight (poker) to draw the missing card to make up a straight (five successive cards: e.g., 6, 7, 8, 9, 10)
maldita sea tu suerto (Spanish) your luck be damned
greaseball (slang, offensive unless meant humorously) a Latin American (because their hair is supposedly oily, greasy; more often called "greaser")
prodigious [prəˈdɪdʒəs] (formal) enormously
elated joyful and happy, full of high spirits
Salerno town in southern Italy, where American forces landed in World War II (1943) and suffered heavy losses
rat-race the never-ending struggle to be better and more successful than others
brag to talk boastfully (in a proud way about one's own achievements)
callous unfeeling
stool seat that has three or four legs, but no back or arms (Careful! "*Stuhl*" is "chair" in English.)

bouclé (French) wool, silk or cotton cloth that has a knotted texture
crushed *zerknittert*
lapel [lə'pel] the front part of a jacket that is joined to the collar and folded back on each side
accessories [ək'sesəriz] articles worn to complete one's dress
is the coast clear? is there any hindrance or danger?
amber brownish yellow (from amber: *Bernstein*)
radiance brightness and beauty
sag to sink down
dissolve [dɪ'zɔlv] (here) to disappear (his gaze is no longer focused)
come to to wake up, to become conscious again

STELLA Yes.

BLANCHE That cool yellow silk – the bouclé. See if it's crushed. If it's not too crushed I'll wear it and on the lapel that silver and turquoise pin in the shape of a seahorse. You will find them in the heart-shaped box I keep my accessories in. And Stella ... Try and locate a bunch of artificial violets in that box, too, to pin with the seahorse on the lapel of the jacket. [*She closes the door. Stella turns to Eunice.*]

STELLA I don't know if I did the right thing.

EUNICE What else could you do?

STELLA I couldn't believe her story and go on living with Stanley.

EUNICE Don't ever believe it. Life has got to go on. No matter what happens, you've got to keep on going. [*The bathroom door opens a little.*]

BLANCHE [*looking out*] Is the coast clear?

STELLA Yes, Blanche. [*To Eunice*] Tell her how well she's looking.

BLANCHE Please close the curtains before I come out.

STELLA They're closed.

STANLEY – How many for you?

PABLO – Two.

STEVE – Three.

[*Blanche appears in the amber light of the door. She has a tragic radiance in her red satin robe following the sculptural lines of her body. The "Varsouviana" rises audibly as Blanche enters the bedroom.*]

BLANCHE [*with faintly hysterical vivacity*] I have just washed my hair.

STELLA Did you?

BLANCHE I'm not sure I got the soap out.

EUNICE Such fine hair!

BLANCHE [*accepting the compliment*] It's a problem. Didn't I get a call?

STELLA Who from, Blanche?

BLANCHE Shep Huntleigh ...

STELLA Why, not yet, honey!

BLANCHE How strange! I –

[*At the sound of Blanche's voice Mitch's arm supporting his cards has sagged and his gaze is dissolved into space. Stanley slaps him on the shoulder.*]

STANLEY Hey, Mitch, come to!

[*The sound of this new voice shocks Blanche. She makes a shocked gesture, forming his name with her lips. Stella nods and looks quickly away. Blanche stands quite still for some moments – the silverbacked mirror in her hand and a look of sorrowful perplexity as though all human experience shows on her face. Blanche finally speaks but with sudden hysteria.*]

BLANCHE What's going on here?

[*She turns from Stella to Eunice and back to Stella. Her rising voice penetrates the concentration of the game. Mitch ducks his head lower but Stanley shoves back his chair as if about to rise. Steve places a restraining hand on his arm.*]

BLANCHE [*continuing*] What's happened here? I want an explanation of what's happened here.

STELLA [*agonizingly*] Hush! Hush!

EUNICE Hush! Hush! Honey.

STELLA Please, Blanche.

BLANCHE Why are you looking at me like that? Is something wrong with me?

EUNICE You look wonderful, Blanche. Don't she look wonderful?

STELLA Yes.

EUNICE I understand you are going on a trip.

STELLA Yes, Blanche is. She's going on a vacation.

EUNICE I'm green with envy.

BLANCHE Help me, help me get dressed!

STELLA [*handing her dress*] Is this what you –

BLANCHE Yes, it will do! I'm anxious to get out of here – this place is a trap!

EUNICE What a pretty blue jacket.

STELLA It's lilac colored.

BLANCHE You're both mistaken. It's Della Robbia blue. The blue of the robe in the old Madonna pictures. Are these grapes washed?

[*She fingers the bunch of grapes which Eunice had brought in.*]

EUNICE Huh?

BLANCHE Washed, I said. Are they washed?

EUNICE They're from the French Market.

BLANCHE That doesn't mean they've been washed. [*The cathedral bells chime*] Those cathedral bells – they're the only clean thing in the Quarter. Well, I'm going now. I'm ready to go.

EUNICE [*whispering*] She's going to walk out before they get here.

STELLA Wait, Blanche.

BLANCHE I don't want to pass in front of those men.

EUNICE Then wait'll the game breaks up.

STELLA Sit down and ...

[*Blanche turns weakly, hesitantly about. She lets them push her into a chair.*]

BLANCHE I can smell the sea air. The rest of my time I'm going to spend on the sea. And when I die, I'm going to die on the

---

perplexity bewilderment, confusion

restrain to check, to hold back from action

agonizing ['ægənaɪzɪŋ] in great mental or physical pain

What has happened between Scenes 10 and 11? You may imagine a scene between Blanche and Stella or Stanley and Stella and invent a suitable dialogue. What may have been Tennessee Williams's reasons for not writing such a scene?

lilac ['laɪlək] a shrub or tree with blossoms ranging in colour from white to lavender

Della Robbia blue intense blue colour named after the Florentine sculptor Luca Della Robbia (1400–1482), whose preferred colour it was

chime to ring (bell or clock)

hesitant slow to act because one feels uncertain
to hesitate, hesitation

mustache [mə'stɑːʃ], AE ['mʌstæʃ] the hair growing on a man's upper lip
quinine ['kwaɪnaɪn] *Chinin*

sea. You know what I shall die of? [*She plucks a grape*] I shall die of eating an unwashed grape one day out on the ocean. I will die – with my hand in the hand of some nice-looking ship's doctor, a very young one with a small blond mustache and a big silver watch. "Poor lady," they'll say, "the quinine did her no good. That unwashed grape has transported her soul to heaven." [*The cathedral chimes are heard*] And I'll be buried at sea sewn up in a clean white sack and dropped overboard – at noon – in the blaze of summer – and into an ocean as blue as [*Chimes again*] my first lover's eyes!

Matron ['meɪtrən] (old-fashioned) senior nurse
gravity seriousness

detachment the state of not being emotionally interested; aloofness

[*A Doctor and a Matron have appeared around the corner of the building and climbed the steps to the porch. The gravity of their profession is exaggerated – the unmistakable aura of the state institution with its cynical detachment. The Doctor rings the doorbell. The murmur of the game is interrupted.*]

EUNICE [*whispering to Stella*] That must be them.

[*Stella presses her fists to her lips.*]

BLANCHE [*rising slowly*] What is it?

EUNICE [*affectedly casual*] Excuse me while I see who's at the door.

STELLA Yes.

[*Eunice goes into the kitchen.*]

BLANCHE [*tensely*] I wonder if it's for me.

colloquy conference, conversation

[*A whispered colloquy takes place at the door.*]

EUNICE [*returning, brightly*] Someone is calling for Blanche.

Comment on Blanche's self-delusion. Show how she has gradually lost touch with reality ➔

BLANCHE It *is* for me, then! [*She looks fearfully from one to the other and then to the portieres. The "Varsouviana" faintly plays*] Is it the gentleman I was expecting from Dallas?

EUNICE I think it is, Blanche.

BLANCHE I'm not quite ready.

STELLA Ask him to wait outside.

BLANCHE I ...

[*Eunice goes back to the portieres. Drums sound very softly.*]

STELLA Everything packed?

BLANCHE My silver toilet articles are still out.

STELLA Ah!

EUNICE [*returning*] They're waiting in front of the house.

BLANCHE They! Who's "they"?

EUNICE There's a lady with him.

BLANCHE I cannot imagine who this "lady" could be! How is she dressed?

plain-tailored outfit plain, simple clothes

EUNICE Just – just a sort of a – plain-tailored outfit.

BLANCHE Possibly she's – [*Her voice dies out nervously.*]

STELLA Shall we go, Blanche?

BLANCHE Must we go through that room?

Stella I will go with you.

Blanche How do I look?

Stella Lovely.

Eunice [*echoing*] Lovely.

[*Blanche moves fearfully to the portieres. Eunice draws them open for her. Blanche goes into the kitchen.*]

Blanche [*to the men*] Please don't get up. I'm only passing through.

[*She crosses quickly to outside door. Stella and Eunice follow. The poker players stand awkwardly at the table – all except Mitch, who remains seated, looking down at the table. Blanche steps out on a small porch at the side of the door. She stops short and catches her breath.*]

Doctor How do you do?

Blanche You are not the gentleman I was expecting. [*She suddenly gasps and starts back up the steps. She stops by Stella, who stands just outside the door, and speaks in a frightening whisper*] That man isn't Shep Huntleigh.

[*The "Varsouviana" is playing distantly.*]

[*Stella stares back at Blanche. Eunice is holding Stella's arm. There is a moment of silence – no sound but that of Stanley steadily shuffling the cards.*]

[*Blanche catches her breath again and slips back into the flat. She enters the flat with a peculiar smile, her eyes wide and brilliant. As soon as her sister goes past her, Stella closes her eyes and clenches her hands. Eunice throws her arms comfortingly about her. Then she starts up to her flat. Blanche stops just inside the door. Mitch keeps staring down at his hands on the table, but the other men look at her curiously. At last she starts around the table toward the bedroom. As she does, Stanley suddenly pushes back his chair and rises as if to block her way. The Matron follows her into the flat.*]

porch a structure attached to the entrance of a building that has a roof (also called "veranda" or "verandah")

How do you respond to Stella in this scene? Does she grow in stature or does she lose the audience's sympathy?

clench to grip closely and hold tightly

comforting ['kʌmfətɪŋ] soothing; encouraging sb who is sad or in distress

The matron and the doctor. From Elia Kazan's film

STANLEY Did you forget something?

BLANCHE [*shrilly*] Yes! Yes, I forgot something!

[*She rushes past him into the bedroom. Lurid reflections appear on the walls in odd, sinuous shapes. The "Varsouviana" is filtered into a weird distortion, accompanied by the cries and noises of the jungle. Blanche seizes the back of a chair as if to defend herself.*]

STANLEY [*sotto voce*] Doc, you better go in.

DOCTOR [*sotto voce, motioning to the Matron*] Nurse, bring her out.

[*The Matron advances on one side, Stanley on the other. Divested of all the softer properties of womanhood, the Matron is a peculiarly sinister figure in her severe dress. Her voice is bold and toneless as a firebell.*]

MATRON Hello, Blanche.

[*The greeting is echoed and re-echoed by other mysterious voices behind the walls, as if reverberated through a canyon of rock.*]

STANLEY She says that she forgot something.

[*The echo sounds in threatening whispers.*]

MATRON That's all right.

STANLEY What did you forget, Blanche?

BLANCHE I – I –

MATRON It don't matter. We can pick it up later.

STANLEY Sure. We can send it along with the trunk.

BLANCHE [*retreating in panic*] I don't know you – I don't know you. I want to be – left alone – please!

MATRON Now, Blanche!

ECHOES [*rising and falling*] Now, Blanche – now, Blanche – now, Blanche!

STANLEY You left nothing here but spilt talcum and old empty perfume bottles – unless it's the paper lantern you want to take with you. You want the lantern?

[*He crosses to dressing table and seizes the paper lantern, tearing it off the light bulb, and extends it toward her. She cries out as if the lantern was herself. The Matron steps boldly toward her. She screams and tries to break past the Matron. All the men spring to their feet. Stella runs out to the porch, with Eunice following to comfort her, simultaneously with the confused voices of the men in the kitchen. Stella rushes into Eunice's embrace on the porch.*]

STELLA Oh, my God, Eunice help me! Don't let them do that to her, don't let them hurt her! Oh, God, oh, please God, don't hurt her! What are they doing to her? What are they doing? [*She tries to break from Eunice's arms.*]

EUNICE No, honey, no, no, honey. Stay here. Don't go back in there. Stay with me and don't look.

weird strange, bizarre
distortion the state of being twisted out of shape; the unfaithful reproduction of a sound
sotto voce (Italian) in an undertone
motion to make a movement (with one's head or hands) to show sb what they are to do
divested of (formal) stripped of, without
property characteristic quality

reverberate to echo, to repeat several times
canyon (AE) a long, narrow valley between high cliffs

talcum ['tælkəm] a powder for the face and body, usually perfumed

How do you evaluate ➔ Stanley's actions here? What do they show? Callousness, indifference, relief, covert unease, remorse? Compare his actions here with his words to Stella at the end of the play. Also, compare his actions with those of Mitch.

simultaneous [ˌsɪməl'teɪniəs], AE [saɪməl] happening at the same time

STELLA What have I done to my sister? Oh, God, what have I done to my sister?

EUNICE You done the right thing, the only thing you could do. She couldn't stay here; there wasn't no other place for her to go.

[*While Stella and Eunice are speaking on the porch the voices of the men in the kitchen overlap them. Mitch has started toward the bedroom. Stanley crosses to block him. Stanley pushes him aside. Mitch lunges and strikes at Stanley. Stanley pushes Mitch back. Mitch collapses at the table, sobbing.*]

[*During the preceding scenes, the Matron catches hold of Blanche's arm and prevents her flight. Blanche turns wildly and scratches at the Matron. The heavy woman pinions her arms. Blanche cries out hoarsely and slips to her knees.*]

MATRON These fingernails have to be trimmed. [*The Doctor comes into the room and she looks at him.*] Jacket, Doctor?

DOCTOR Not unless necessary.

[*He takes off his hat and now he becomes personalized. The unhuman quality goes. His voice is gentle and reassuring as he crosses to Blanche and crouches in front of her. As he speaks her name, her terror subsides a little. The lurid reflections fade from the walls, the inhuman cries and noises die out and her own hoarse crying is calmed.*]

DOCTOR Miss DuBois.

[*She turns her face to him and stares at him with desperate pleading. He smiles; then he speaks to the Matron.*]

It won't be necessary.

BLANCHE [*faintly*] Ask her to let go of me.

DOCTOR [*to the Matron*] Let go.

[*The Matron releases her. Blanche extends her hands toward the Doctor. He draws her up gently and supports her with his arm and leads her through the portieres.*]

BLANCHE [*holding tight to his arm*] Whoever you are – I have always depended on the kindness of strangers.

[*The poker players stand back as Blanche and the Doctor cross the kitchen to the front door. She allows him to lead her as if she were blind. As they go out on the porch, Stella cries out her sister's name from where she is crouched a few steps up on the stairs.*]

STELLA Blanche! Blanche, Blanche!

[*Blanche walks on without turning, followed by the Doctor and the Matron. They go around the corner of the building.*]

[*Eunice descends to Stella and places the child in her arms. It is wrapped in a pale blue blanket. Stella accepts the child, sobbingly. Eunice continues downstairs and enters the kitchen where*

overlap to extend over a part of another thing

lunge to make a sudden movement towards sb so as to attack them

trim to cut short

jacket (here) a straitjacket (jacket used to restrain a person in a violent or hysterical state)

What do the stage directions say about the doctor's change of demeanour? What does this change suggest? Compare the doctor's conduct with that of the matron.

became personalized to become like a real person

subside to become less intense

Do Blanche's words, "I have always depended on the kindness of strangers", fairly sum up her whole life? Has she always been a victim, or has she also been a victimizer? Why doesn't the play end with Blanche being led away by the doctor?

the men, except for Stanley, are returning silently to their places about the table. Stanley has gone out on the porch and stands at the foot of the steps looking at Stella.]

STANLEY [*a bit uncertainly*] Stella?

[*She sobs with inhuman abandon. There is something luxurious in her complete surrender to crying now that her sister is gone.*]

STANLEY [*voluptuously, soothingly*] Now, honey. Now, love. Now, now, love. [*He kneels beside her and his fingers find the opening of her blouse*] Now, now, love. Now, love ...

[*The luxurious sobbing, the sensual murmur fade away under the swelling music of the "blue piano" and the muted trumpet.*]

STEVE This game is seven-card stud.

CURTAIN

with inhuman abandon without control over her emotions
surrender the act of giving up and accepting what has happened
voluptuous [vəˈlʌptʃuəs] characterised by the promise of sensual pleasure
soothing [ˈsuːðɪŋ] making calm by gentle treatment
muted (of a sound or an instrument) softened, muffled, less loud

"I have always depended on the kindness of strangers." Fron Elia Kazan's film

Additional Material

Tennessee Williams: A Timeline

Tennessee Williams

Lanier [lə'nɪə]

audit (AE) to attend a university course without intending to get a credit for it

itinerant [aɪ'tɪnərənt] travelling from place to place

extension course (university) a course for people who are not full-time students

March 26, 1911: Thomas Lanier Williams III is born in Columbus, Mississippi (friends later call him Tennessee due to his deep Southern accent), but in 1918 his family moves to St. Louis, Missouri.

1929: He attends classes at the University of Missouri-Columbia. He audits a course on drama and writes his first one-act play. He is influenced by the poet Hart Crane, the Norwegian dramatist Henrik Ibsen and the Russian dramatist Anton Chekhov. He does not finish his schooling but leads an itinerant life and, for a time, works as a clerk at a shoe company.

1936: He enrols in extension courses at Washington University, St. Louis, trying his hand at plays which are produced by local drama groups.

1937: He transfers to the University of Iowa, from which he graduates with a degree in English.

1939: He moves to New Orleans, where he lives in the French Quarter. He officially adopts his nickname Tennessee and continues writing stories and plays.

1940: His first full-length play, *Battle of Angels,* fails dismally in Boston.

dismal bad and unsuccessful, miserable

1944: *The Glass Menagerie* opens in Chicago. It is his first major success. The play is based on a screenplay, *The Gentleman Caller,* drafted while working for Metro Goldwyn Mayer in Hollywood.

to draft to write a first sketch that needs to be reworked later

Dec. 3, 1947: *A Streetcar Named Desire* opens on Broadway, directed by Elia Kazan and starring Jessica Tandy, Marlon Brando, Kim Hunter and Karl Malden. The play wins him his first Pulitzer Prize for Drama. It is a reworked dramatic sketch, *The Poker Night,* which he writes while living in the French Quarter.

1948: *Summer and Smoke,* which is no great success with theatregoers.

1950: His major novel *The Roman Spring of Mrs. Stone* (also filmed) is published.

1951: *The Rose Tattoo* wins the Tony Award for Best Play of the Year (the film version wins Anna Magnani an Academy Award in 1955).
Elia Kazan directs his famous film *A Streetcar Named Desire* (included in the selection of the 100 Best American Films), which turns Marlon Brando into a movie mega star and wins Vivien Lee, Kim Hunter and Karl Malden Academy Awards (there are two further versions of the play, both written for TV: one starring Ann-Margret and Treat Williams, 1984, the other Jessica Lange and Alec Baldwin, 1995).

vitriolic sharp and bitter, biting

1953: *Camino Real* opens on Broadway but, due to vitriolic critiques, closes after only two months.

1954: *Cat on a Hot Tin Roof* opens on Broadway, directed by Elia Kazan (in 1958, a famous film version, starring Paul Newman and Elizabeth Taylor, is released to great acclaim).

acclaim applause, praise

1955: The film *Baby Doll,* based on a screenplay by Tennessee Williams, is blacklisted by the Catholic Church.

to blacklist to make a list of people or things that should be avoided and remain unsupported

downturn a downward trend

debut ['deɪbju] to appear in public for the first time

1957: *Orpheus Descending,* a reworking of *Battle of Angels,* debuts on Broadway.

1958: *Suddenly Last Summer* (another controversial play; filmed in 1959).

1959: *Sweet Bird of Youth* opens on Broadway but runs for only three months.

1960: *A Period of Adjustment,* an uncharacteristic comedy, runs for over four months.

1961: Williams becomes increasingly dependent on drugs as his career takes a downturn.

1962: Film versions *of Sweet Bird of Youth* and *A Period of Adjustment* are released.
The failure of *The Milk Train Doesn't Stop Here Anymore* signals his inexorable decline. His problems are compounded by the death from lung cancer of Frank Merlo, his friend of many years, which leaves him depressed and forlorn.
Humanities Degree by the University of Missouri and a Medal for Drama by the American Academy of Arts and Letters.

to compound to make a difficult situation worse by adding further difficulties

forlorn in pitiful condition, wretched, miserable

1971: He speaks out against the American involvement in Vietnam.

1972: *Small Craft Warnings,* which critics regard as a return to his former skills, opens off Broadway.

1977: After receiving further awards and honorary degrees he returns to New Orleans as the setting for a play, *Vieux Carré,* in which he overtly addresses the subject of homosexuality. The play, however, is another failure with theatre audiences.

honorary degree ['onərəri] a degree given as an honour in recognition of literary or academic distinction

1979: He is presented with a Lifetime Achievement Award in Washington by President Jimmy Carter.

1980: *Clothes for a Summer Hotel,* his last Broadway play, closes after only 15 performances.

1982: He receives an honorary doctorate from Harvard.

February 24, 1983: He is found dead in his room in the Hotel Elysee in New York. He is determined to have died from choking on a plastic bottle cap. He is later buried in St. Louis.

to choke to be suffocated, to be unable to breathe because something blocks your windpipe

New Orleans: A Timeline

1682: French explorers, among them the Sieur de La Salle, arrive at the mouth of the Mississippi River; they claim the region for France and call it Louisiana.

1718: The Sieur de Bienville founds the city of New Orleans.

1763: The Treaty of Paris, which ends the Seven Years' War, results in Spain taking possession of Louisiana.

1800: France reacquires Louisiana from Spain.

1803: The United States buys the Louisiana Territory from France for about $ 15 million and thus more than doubles its size (the Louisiana Purchase).

1812: Louisiana is admitted to the Union.

1814: In the Battle of New Orleans General Andrew Jackson and his forces defeat the British.

1840: The country's oldest family-run restaurant, Antoine's, opens in New Orleans.

1853: Yellow fever decimates the population of New Orleans.

1857: The first modern-style festival of Mardi Gras.

1862: After secession from the Union in the Civil War, New Orleans is captured by Union troops and held till the end of the war.

1868: Louisiana is readmitted to the Union (its new constitution grants voting rights to black males and integrates its public schools and institutions).

1890: The segregation of railway cars becomes law in Louisiana.

1890: Ferdinand "Jelly Roll" Morton, generally considered the first jazz composer and pianist, is born in Louisiana.

1896: The U.S. Court delivers the Plessy v. Ferguson decision allowing racial segregation in Louisiana (in 1892, Homer Plessy, who is categorized as "coloured", boards a train in New Orleans although it is reserved for whites; he is arrested but fights the charge all the way to the Supreme Court).

1901: Louis Armstrong is born in New Orleans. He will later be called "the father of jazz".

to reacquire to buy or get back

purchase ['pɜːtʃəs] land etc. acquired by buying

to integrate (AE) to remove the legal and social barriers imposing segregation on ethnic groups

segregation the policy of compelling ethnic groups to live apart from each other

charge accusation

1905: Another outbreak of yellow fever.

charter a written grant of legal rights made by a government

1912: A charter is granted to Loyola University in New Orleans.

1921: A commission is formed to preserve the Vieux Carré (also called the French Quarter).

1927: Continual rainfall causes disastrous flooding.

1938: Tennessee Williams arrives in the French Quarter, which is to become the setting of several of his plays.

1949: Louis Armstrong is celebrated in his home town as "King of the Mardi Gras".

1954: The Supreme Court in the Brown v. Board of Education decision revokes the Plessy v. Ferguson decision.

to revoke to cancel or annul (a law or a permission)

1960: The first black student enters the William Frantz Public Elementary School in New Orleans amidst white protest and turmoil.

turmoil tumult, uproar

1961: Preservation Hall opens; it is intended as a living museum dedicated to New Orleans' heritage of jazz.

1962: Tulane University admits black students.

1965: Hurricane Betsy causes widespread flooding and the death of dozens of residents.

1970: New Orleans hosts the first of its nine Super Bowls, the national Football League's championship game.

to host to provide a place and the logistics for an event (sports, politics etc.)

1978: Ernest Morial becomes the first black mayor of New Orleans.

1987: Pope John Paul II visits New Orleans.

2005: Hurricane Katrina strikes the city: levees are breached and portions of the city flooded. Residents are evacuated and large sections remain under water until the water levels begin to drop in September. More than 1,600 people are killed, and even more become homeless.

levee ['levi] (AE) an embankment built alongside a river to prevent high water from flooding bordering land
breach (water) to break open or through

2006: The rebuilding of New Orleans begins.

Mel Leavitt: Melting Pot

New Orleans is a large metropolitan city, an international port and a "melting pot" of many races und cultures. It is also a remarkable collection of historic neighborhoods, many of them as separate and distinctive as if they were separate townships or small villages.

[...] New Orleans is essentially an "island." [...] It is squeezed between the Mississippi River and the nation's seventh largest lake (Pontchartrain), surrounded on all sides by a giant oak-cypress swamp. Napoleon Bonaparte referred to it as the Isle d'Orléans. Early French settlers called it "leflotant," the floating land.

As such, Island Orleans was both isolated und insulated from the mainland for almost 250 years. Thus, it was able to develop, without threat of dissimulation, its own unique cultural innovations: jazz, Creole cuisine, Mardi Gras, above ground burial sites ("cities of the dead"), cultural rites (including the famous jazz funerals) that resisted the homogenization that depersonalized many American cities in the 20th century.

[...] Until 1890, the area was a collective of disconnected suburbs – neighborhoods without neighbors. In many cases they were divided by language. The original French Creoles spoke French and disdained the "Americans" who arrived 90 years later. The Germans, Irish, Italians, West Indians added up to the "unbelievable babble of a dozen languages and scores of dialects in the city's marketplaces."

[...] The attachment to neighborhood remains so strong that many third and fourth generation residents take pride in living in their "grandfather's house." In addition, many neighborhoods (some dating back to 1800) have maintained much historical character, with ten now listed as National Historic Districts. The Uptown Historic District is the second largest in the USA with over 10,000 structures. The largest downtown Historic district, Esplanade Ridge, lies just below the French Quarter, home of the "last Creole aristocrats."

distinctive characteristic; that which makes sb or sth clearly distinct from others
township in the USA, a division of a county, constituting a unit of local government with administrative control of schools, roads etc.

to insulate to keep sb or sth apart from unpleasant experiences or influences

Creole ['kriːəul] (here) a person descended from the original French settlers of Louisiana
homogenization [həˌmɒdʒənaɪ'zeɪʃn] making uniform
to depersonalize to cause sb to lose their sense of identity

to disdain to regard as unworthy; to reject with contempt
babble meaningless or confused and incoherent talk

structure (here) a building

How to Be a Southern Belle

to strive to endeavour, to try hard

Mint Julep (AE) a frosted drink consisting of bourbon or brandy, sugar, mint leaves und crushed ice

grits (AE) corn or soybeans ground more coarsely than for flour or meal, usually eaten as porridge

to expend to spend a lot of energy on

expired (here) exhausted ("to expire" is to breathe one's last breath)

kegger (AE, dialect) a loud and boisterous party

cotillion [kəˈtɪliən] a formal dance at which debutantes are presented (originally, a cotillion is a lively dance)

garbage any worthless or offensive matter

country club a social club, usually on the outskirts of a city, with a clubhouse, golf course und other facilities

magnolia a tree with large fragrant flowers of white, pink or purple (the magnolia tree is something like an emblem of the South)

parasol a lightweight umbrella carried by women as a sunshade

girdle a woman's undergarment moulding her waist und hips und designed to make her appear slimmer

All Southern women strive to be belles.
Here's how:

1. Offer Mint Julep or Iced Tea to everyone who visits your house.
2. Eat grits every day for breakfast.
3. Refer to your house as "The Plantation" no matter how small your house may be.
4. Refer to all men as "gentlemen callers" or "beaux".
5. Never let a man know you're interested or chase him because you know there are too many men who want you for you to expend the extra effort.
6. When you have a dating dilemma und have one gentleman caller over when you are expecting another, claim to be "expired" und excuse yourself for a nap until he leaves.
7. Whenever you are asked to do any work, fan yourself and claim to have the "vapors."
8. Refer to every party you go to, even a kegger at the local university, as a "cotillion." All other parties are yankee garbage.
9. Try to use words like "darling", "sweet" or "precious" in every sentence.
10. Belong to a country club. If you don't, refer to any club you belong to as a "country club". No one will know the difference.
11. Sit under a magnolia tree with a parasol fanning yourself often. Passers-by will take notice of your belle-ness.
12. Never marry a Yankee unless you want to be a Yankee by association.
13. Never be seen without your makeup und girdle.

Tips:

1. A parasol und an umbrella are not the same thing. If you refer to your parasol as an "umbrelly" you will never be a belle.
2. Being a belle is a lifetime of work; so practice every day.

Michel-Guillaume Jean de Crèvecœur: What is an American?

What attachment can a poor European emigrant have for a country where he had nothing? The knowledge of the language, the love of a few kindred as poor as himself, were the only cords that tied him; his country is now that which gives him his land, bread, protection, and consequence; *Ubi panis ibi patria* is the motto of all emigrants. What, then, is the American, this new man? He is neither an European, nor the descendant of an European; hence that strange mixture of blood, which you will find in no other country. I could point out to you a family whose grandfather was an Englishman, whose wife was Dutch, whose son married a French woman, and whose present four sons have now four wives of different nations. *He* is an American, who, leaving behind him all his ancient prejudices and manners, receives new ones from the new mode of life he has embraced, the new government he obeys, and the new rank he holds. He becomes an American by being received in the broad lap of our great Alma Mater. Here individuals of all nations are melted into a new race of men, whose labours and posterity will one day cause great changes in the world. Americans are the western pilgrims who are carrying along with them that great mass of arts, sciences, vigour, and industry which began long since in the East; they will finish the great circle. The Americans were once scattered all over Europe; here they are incorporated into one of the finest systems of population which has ever appeared, and which will hereafter become distinct by the power of the different climates they inhabit. The American ought therefore to love his country much better than that wherein either he or his forefathers were born. Here the rewards of his industry follow with equal steps the progress of his labour; his labour is founded on the basis of nature, self-interest; can it want a stronger allurement? Wives and children, who before in vain demanded of him a morsel of bread, now, fat and frolicsome, gladly help their father to clear those fields when exuberant crops are to arise to feed and to clothe them all, without any part being claimed, either by a despotic prince, a rich abbot, or a mighty lord. Here religion demands but little of him: a small voluntary salary to the

attachment affection, love

kindred relatives or family; kinfolk

consequence importance

ubi panis ibi patria (Latin) my country is where I earn my daily bread

descendant sb who is the offspring of sb who lived a long time ago (*Nachkomme*)

to embrace (here) to take up eagerly, to adopt

Alma Mater [ˌælməˈmɑːtə] (Latin) fostering mother (often used to denote the school or college one attended)

posterity all succeeding generations

the great circle a reference to a once accepted theory that civilization moves westward with the sun; starting in Asia, civilization and power were transferred to Rome and other empires and via Britain finally reached America, which would conquer the continent and reach the Pacific Ocean and, finally, Asia (the theory is also called "translatio imperii")

industry steady effort and application to work

allurement [əˈlʊəmənt] temptation; fascination

morsel a small piece; a small bite of food

frolicsome (old-fashioned) full of high spirits, playful and happy

exuberant [ɪɡˈzjuːbərənt] (here) plentiful

minister and gratitude to God; can he refuse these? The American is a new man, who acts upon new principles; he must therefore entertain new ideas and form new opinions. From involuntary idleness, servile dependence, penury, and useless labour, he has passed to toils of a very different nature, rewarded by ample subsistence. This is an American.

idleness ['aɪdlnəs] inactivity, not being employed in work
servile ['sɜːvaɪl], AE ['sɜːvl] like a slave or servant
penury ['penjəri] extreme poverty
toil hard work
ample more than enough, abundant
subsistence livelihood, sb's means of support

What is the American Dream?

The term was first used by James Truslow Adams in his book *The Epic of America* which was written in 1931. He states: "The American Dream is that dream of a land in which life should be better and richer and fuller for everyone, with opportunity for each according to ability or achievement. It is a difficult dream for the European upper classes to interpret adequately, and too many of us ourselves have grown weary and mistrustful of it. It is not a dream of motor cars and high wages merely, but a dream of social order in which each man and each woman shall be able to attain to the fullest stature of which they are innately capable, and be recognized by others for what they are, regardless of the fortuitous circumstances of birth or position."

In the United States Declaration of Independence, our founding fathers: "... held certain truths to be self-evident, that all Men are created equal, that they are endowed by their Creator with certain unalienable Rights, that among these are Life, Liberty and the Pursuit of Happiness." [...]

Were homesteaders who left the big cities of the east to find happiness and their piece of land in the unknown wilderness pursuing these inalienable Rights? Were the immigrants who came to the United States looking for their bit of life, liberty and the pursuit of happiness, their Dream? [...] Is the American Dream attainable by all Americans? [...]

Some say, that the American Dream has become the pursuit of material prosperity – that people work more hours to get bigger cars, fancier homes, the fruits of prosperity for their families – but have less time to enjoy their prosperity. Others say that the American Dream is beyond the grasp of the working poor who must work two jobs to insure their family's survival. Yet others look toward a new American Dream with less focus on financial gain and more emphasis on living a simple, fulfilling life.

Thomas Wolfe said, "[...] to every man, regardless of his birth, his shining, golden opportunity [...] the right to live, to work, to be himself, and to become whatever thing his manhood and his vision can combine to make him."

adequate ['ædɪkwət] suitable; good enough for what is required
merely ['mɪəli] only

fortuitous happening by chance, accidental

to endow to provide with, to give
unalienable (also, inalienable) that may not be taken away
homesteader (AE) a settler who holds a homestead granted by the U.S. government (generally, the word refers to a settler who, in the wake of the so-called Homestead Act of 1862, which granted 160 acres to a person willing to settle in the then wild and undeveloped trans-Mississippi West, tilled the soil and developed it as a farm)
attainable (formal) that which can be achieved
fancy expensive and fashionable (often having a lot of decorations and complicated patterns)
prosperity wealth and success

Charles Spencer: *A Streetcar named Desire* with Rachel Weisz, at the Donmar Warehouse

Great play though it undoubtedly is, Tennessee Williams's *A Streetcar named Desire* (1947) is an exceptionally tough nut to crack.

The mixture of brutal realism and haunting stage poetry can make for grinding, dramatic gear changes, and the role of Blanche DuBois has defeated many a celebrated actress. Over the years I have seen Jessica Lange, Glenn Close, and the late Natasha Richardson attempt to come to terms with Blanche's extraordinary poignancy, variety and depth, and fine actresses though they are, or were, none quite penetrated its heart.

haunting sad and beautiful at the same time and likely to linger on

grinding [aɪ] (noise) unpleasant as a result of parts of machinery rubbing together

poignancy ['pɔɪnjənsi] sth that is painful to the feelings and evokes compassion

To be frank, I thought Rachel Weisz would almost certainly fail to rise to the challenge. She has had relatively little stage experience and surely, I reasoned, she was too young, and too beautiful, to play the now fading, hard-drinking and wildly promiscuous Southern belle on the edge of complete breakdown.

In fact she rises to the challenge magnificently. It's worth pointing out that Williams's own stage directions described the character as being about 30. Her undoubted beauty is combined here with a fluttering, birdlike nervousness, and sudden moments of desperate panic, that wrench the heart. Better yet, she seems pitifully tiny and vulnerable in comparison with Elliot Cowan as a big, brutal and spectacularly muscular Stanley Kowalski. Watching these two together is like watching an untamed beast cruelly toying with its prey.

promiscuous engaging in sexual intercourse with many persons

magnificent beautiful in a grand and stately way; exceptionally good

fluttering being in a state of restless excitement (originally said of birds: flapping their wings rapidly in excitement)

to wrench (here) to hurt (originally, to pull sth rapidly or violently from a place where it is being held)

vulnerable easily hurt

The contrast between Weisz's refined and mannered gentility, and Cowan's coarse, destructive physicality creates a simmering tension that keeps you on the edge of your seat throughout.

mannered artificial, affected, stylised

gentility showing affected or excessive refinement and elegance

simmering remaining at or just below boiling point; about to break out (e.g. anger)

The rape scene, in which he shatters what is left of her reason, is almost too painful to watch. But even that is less distressing than the climax in which the grim asylum keepers come to take her away to a future too horrible to contemplate and with heart-catching Southern grace Blanche announces that she has always relied on the kindness of strangers.

distressing causing pain and misery

Rob Ashford directs an intense production that gains greatly from being played in this small, intimate space, and in dreamlike passages the characters from Blanche's past come back to haunt her.

Ruth Wilson is outstanding as Stella, caught between her forgiving and passionate love for Stanley and her deep sisterly feelings for Blanche, while Barnaby Kay moves from gauche gentleness to cruel brutality as the suitor who might just offer Blanche the possibility of salvation.

The show is at times a touch too leisurely, and Weisz could dig even deeper into her character's fear, shame and vulnerability, but this is, by some distance, the best *Streetcar* I have ever seen.

gauche [gəʊʃ] doing sth awkwardly because you do not know how to behave in a given situation
suitor a man who courts a woman
salvation being saved from danger or evil

Tim Dirks: *A Streetcar Named Desire*

steamy (slang) erotic
to adapt to make suitable by changing (a text for a different medium)
Pulitzer Prize (AE) any of a number of yearly prizes established by Joseph Pulitzer (1847–1911), Hungarian-born newspaper owner and philanthropist; given for outstanding works in journalism, music and literature

A Streetcar Named Desire (1951) is a subversive, steamy film classic that was adapted from Tennessee Williams' 1947 Pulitzer Prize-winning play of the same name. [...] Playwright Williams adapted his own play for the screen version. This film masterpiece was directed by independent director Elia Kazan (his first piece of work with Williams), a socially-conscious director who insisted that the film be true to the play

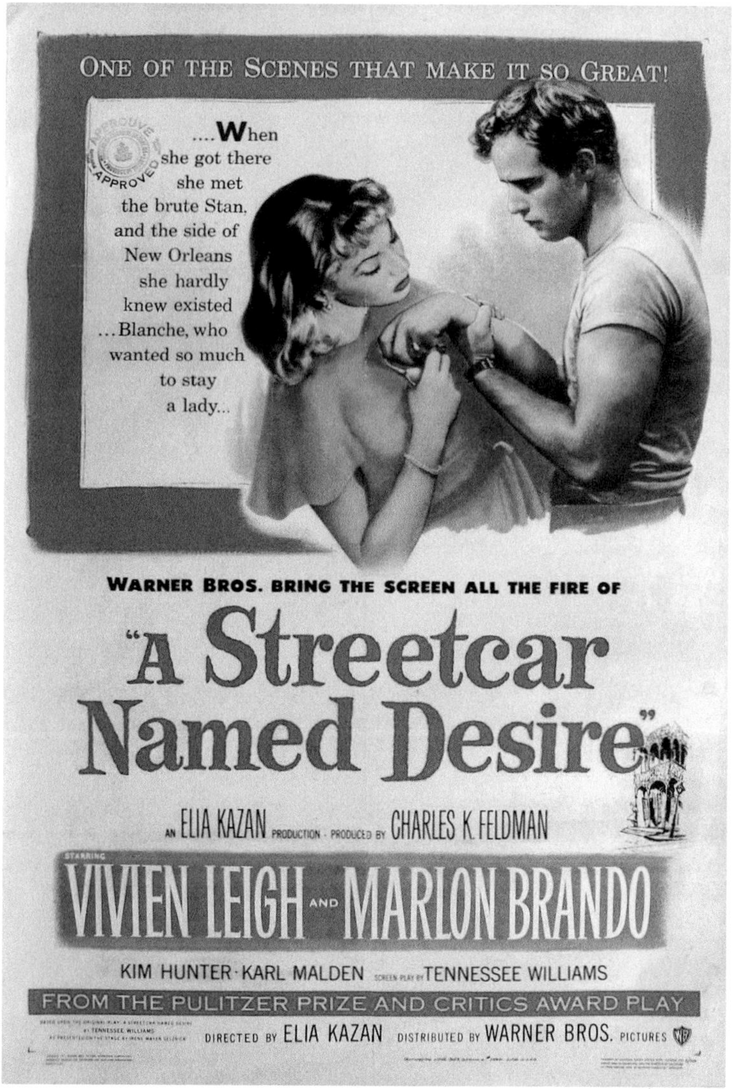

(that he had also directed on Broadway). However, it was opened up to include places only briefly mentioned or non-existent in the play, such as the bowling alley, the pier of a dance casino, and the machine factory.

The electrifying film tells the feverish story of the pathetic mental and emotional demise of a determined, yet fragile, repressed and delicate Southern lady (Blanche) born to a once-wealthy family of Mississippi planters. Her impoverished, tragic downfall in the squalid, cramped and tawdry French Quarter one-bedroom apartment of her married sister (Stella) and animalistic brother-in-law (Stanley) is at the hands of savage, brutal forces in modern society. In her search for refuge, she finds that her sister lives (approvingly) with drunkenness, violence, lust, and ignorance.

This visceral film, considered controversial, decadent, and "morally repugnant", challenged the regulatory Production Code's censors (and the Legion of Decency) with its bold adult drama and sexual subjects (insanity, rape, domestic violence, homosexuality, sexual obsession, and female promiscuity or nymphomania). Ultimately, it signaled the weakening of Hollywood censorship (and groups such as the Catholic Legion of Decency), although a number of scenes were excised, and new dialogue was written. And the Production Code insisted that Stanley be punished for the rape by the loss of his wife's love at the film's conclusion. In 1993, approximately three to five minutes of the censored scenes (i.e., specific references to Blanche's homosexual – or bisexual young husband, her nymphomania, and Stanley's rape of Blanche) were restored in an "original director's version" video re-release. […]

The controversial film was nominated for a phenomenal twelve and awarded four Oscars (an unprecedented three were in the acting categories): Best Actress for Vivien Leigh, and Best Supporting Awards to Kim Hunter and Karl Malden. This was the first time in Academy history that three acting awards were won by a single film (this feat was later repeated by *Network,* 1976). In addition, the Best B/W Art Direction/Set Decoration was given to Richard Day and George James Hopkins for their naturalistically sordid sets. Remarkably, these other eight nominations were all defeated

- Tennessee Williams' Best Screenplay nomination
- Marlon Brando's Best Actor nomination
- Elia Kazan's Best Director nomination
- Harry Stradling's evocative Best B/W Cinematography nomination

demise [dɪ'maɪz] (formal) death
fragile ['frædʒaɪl], AE ['frædʒl] easily broken; physically weak, frail
repressed (psychology) forcing ideas that are painful to the conscious mind into the unconscious
delicate ['dəlɪkət] finely sensitive in feeling and understanding
downfall a sudden fall from prosperity or power
squalid foul and unclean as a result of neglect or unsanitary conditions
tawdry cheap and badly made; also, showing low moral standards
visceral instinctive and emotional rather than intellectual
repugnant [rɪ'pʌgnənt] (formal) distasteful, offensive, very unpleasant
challenge to refuse to accept that sth is correct, acceptable or legal
regulatory setting up rules and regulations
Production Code a set of rules and moral standards that govern the making of films
obsession [əb'seʃən] an extremely unhealthy interest in sth
promiscuity [ˌpromɪ'skjuːəti] the quality of being undiscriminating in the choice of your sexual partners and engaging in sexual intercourse with many persons
nymphomania [ˌnɪmfə'meɪniə] abnormal and uncontrollable desire by a woman for sexual intercourse
to excise to cut out or away
approximately [ə'proksɪmətli] (formal) roughly, about
award a prize
unprecedented [ʌn'presɪdentɪd] having no precedent or parallel; unheard of
Academy (here) the Academy of Motion Picture Arts and Sciences that awards annual Oscars for excellence in the movies
feat an unusually impressive achievement
B/W (film) black and white
sordid depressingly dirty, squalid

ultra-sultry suggesting or expressing extreme passion or lust (originally, "sultry" is "oppressively hot and moist")

- Alex North's Best Score nomination for the ultra-sultry, steamy score
- Norman Levinson's Best Sound Recording nomination
- Lucinda Ballard's Best B/W Costume Design nomination
- and its Best Picture nomination.

Acknowledgements

Texts

Mel Leavitt: "Melting Pot", from: Greater New Orleans Community Data Center, www.gnocdc.org/articles/meltingpot.html [03.11.2009]

"How to be a Southern Belle", http://littlerock.about.com/library/howto/htbelle.htm [03.11.2009]

Michel-Guillaume Jean de Crèvecœur (J. Hector St. John de Crèvecœur): "What is an American?", excerpt from Letter III from *Letters from an American Farmer,* written between 1770 and 1775, published in 1782, in: Giles Gunn (ed.): *Early American Writing,* Penguin, New York 1994, pp. 475–476

"What is the American Dream?", from Library of Congress, http://memory.loc.gov/learn/lessons/97/dream/thedream.html [03.11. 2009]

Charles Spencer: "*A Streetcar Named Desire,* with Rachel Weisz, at the Donmar Warehouse", www.telegraph.co.uk, 29.07.2009 [03.11.2009]

"A Streetcar Named Desire (1951)", review by Tim Dirks, www.filmsite.org [03.11.2009]

Illustrations

© defd: p. 4; ddp images: p. 5; © Warner Bros. Entertainment Inc.: p. 13, 24, 42, 56, 71, 77, 79, 86, 91, 94, 106; © TerraVista/LOOK-foto: p. 20; Whitney Museum of American Art, New York: p. 34; © picture-alliance/Jazzarchiv: p. 69; ullstein bild: p. 95; other illustrations: Verlagsarchiv Schöningh